Science Everywhere 4

SENIOR AUTHORS

Les Asselstine

Rod Peturson

Brendene Barkley

Cynthia Clarke

Sharron Cooke

Dick Coombs

Margaret Gibson

Brian Herrin

Marcia Klein

Elizabeth LeLacheur

Linda Manson

Bob Piccott

Carla Pieterson

Pamela Quigg

Brenda Shynal

Bryan Szumlas

Anna Totten

CONSULTANT: SCIENTIFIC ACCURACY

Arthur Prudham

HARCOURT
BRACE
CANADA

Harcourt Brace & Company, Canada

Toronto • Orlando • San Diego • London • Sydney

Canadian Cataloguing in Publication Data
Asselstine, Les, 1943-
   Science everywhere 4

ISBN 0-7747-0557-4

1. Science — Juvenile literature. 2. Technology — Juvenile literature.
I. Peturson, Rod, 1952-   . II. Title.

Q163.A874 1999   500   C98-932839-2

Project Manager: Julie Kretchman
Researcher/Writer: Jonathan Bocknek
Editors: Lynn Pereira, Mary Reeve
Editorial Assistants: Ian Nussbaum, Brett Savory
Manager of Editorial Services: Nicola Balfour
Senior Production Editor: Karin Fediw
Production Editors: Dianne Broad, Dawn Hunter,
   Mary Knittl, Margot Miller
Permissions Coordinator: Patricia Buckley
Photo Researchers: Mary Rose MacLachlan, Wendy Yano
Production Manager: Sheila Barry
Production Coordinator: Tanya Mossa
Art Direction and Design: Sonya V. Thursby, Opus House Incorporated
Layout: Steve Eby, Brian Lehen, Sonya V. Thursby, Opus House
   Incorporated
Cover Image: John Cancalosi/Peter Arnold

♾ This book was printed in Canada on acid-free paper.
1 2 3 4 5   03 02 01 00 99

Contents

Welcome to Science Everywhere!

We chose the name for this book because we believe you can find science in just about anything you see or do. The activities in this book will help you understand some scientific ideas and show you how to become a better observer. You will learn how to experiment to test your ideas about how things work. You will also learn how to use science to design and build things, and how to record what you have learned about science and share it with others.

In the unit Science Alive, you will learn about life systems. Life systems describe things that are alive and how they depend on one another.

Soundscapes is about sound energy. In that unit you will do experiments to learn how sound energy travels.

You will have a chance to design and build an invention of your own in Inventor's Workshop.

In Light Show, you will learn about light energy. Your experiments will help you learn how light energy travels.

In Earth Lab, you will explore earth science. Earth science describes our planet earth and how it changes.

The first unit, called Start-Up Science, will get you started. You will learn about science and technology, start your science journal, and make a model of something to help explain a scientific idea. In the last unit, called Celebrating Science, you will use what you have learned to design and build something that celebrates science.

Start-Up Science

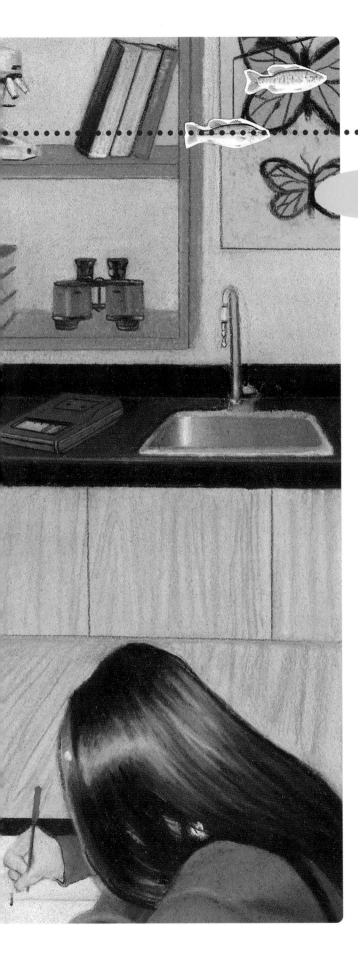

Look around you. Science is every-where. It is in nature—in plants, in animals, and even in us. Science is in our machines and technology, too.

Where is science in this classroom? Where is science in your classroom?

Ask questions. . .
Science and technology discoveries usually begin with a question.

Have you ever wondered. . .

1. why an Arctic hare changes colour?
2. what sound spaceships make in space?
3. how people invent things?
4. what a rainbow is made of?
5. how rocks are formed?

Take a moment to think about these questions. (Scientists ask a lot of questions!) Don't worry if you can't think of some of the answers now. Science is always asking questions, looking for answers, and asking new questions.

Inside Machines

Y ou'd be surprised at the number of everyday objects that are machines. What questions might you ask about these machines?

Each of these machines has gears inside. Gears are wheels with teeth. One gear connects with another gear and turns it. In Getting Started you will examine the gears in a watch. In Let's Investigate you will build a model to show how gears move. In Investigating Further you will make changes to your model to see what effect they have on the gears.

GETTING STARTED

Many machines have gears inside. Cars, grandfather clocks, and Ferris wheels have gears. Look inside this machine to see how the gears work.

The gears inside this watch are very small. As the gears move together the hands of the watch move at the right speed to show the correct time. If you were to listen to this watch you would hear the sound of the moving gears. Tick tock!

LET'S INVESTIGATE

Work with a partner to build a model that shows how gears move.

You will need
- 2 potato slices
- 12 round toothpicks
- 2 pencils
- a marker

1. Gently push the sharpened end of a pencil through each potato slice until about 2 cm of the pencil is showing.

2. Evenly space six toothpicks and insert them into the edges of each potato slice. These slices will become the gears. Write A on one gear and B on the other.

3. Place gear A on the table. Hold the pencil vertically to keep the gear in place.

4. Hold the gear B pencil horizontally so that gear B's toothpicks are between the toothpicks of gear A.

5. Turn gear A to the left or counterclockwise. What happens to gear B? In what direction is gear B moving? What do you notice about how fast the gears are moving?

6. Predict what will happen if gear A is turned to the right. Test your prediction. What do you notice about how fast the gears are moving?

7. Colour a toothpick on each gear. Place both gears so the coloured toothpicks are pointing to 12 o'clock. As you turn gear A until its coloured toothpick returns to 12 o'clock, watch gear B. How many complete turns does gear B make as gear A is turned?

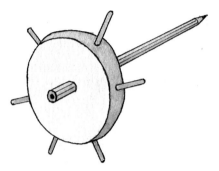

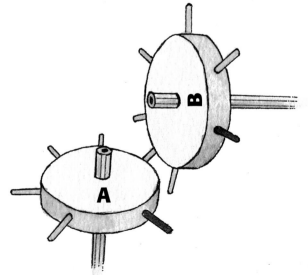

Reflect on Your Results

When gear A was turned, what did you notice about
- its teeth as it met with the teeth of gear B?
- the direction in which the two gears moved?
- the speed of the two gears?
- the number of turns each gear made?

Your Science Journal

Throughout this book you will be asked to write down the things you do in science experiments and the observations you make. You will be asked to record information in different ways—sometimes by making drawings, other times by writing sentences or making charts. If scientists don't keep notes or records of their experiments, their ideas can't be shared with others. A science journal is a good place to keep your notes together.

To get your science journal started, follow these steps:
- Make a title page for your journal by drawing people who use science in their everyday lives. Show at least four different jobs that people do. Share your drawings with your classmates. See if they can figure out what scientific things the people in your drawing have to know.
- On the first page of your journal, start a list of questions that you have about how things work or why things are the way that they are. You will want to add to your list every time you ponder another question. You can start by listing the questions on page 7 and writing what you know about each one in your science journal.
- At the back of your journal, start your own glossary. Start by writing the word **gear**. Write its meaning in your own words and then write a sentence using the word. Every time you come across a word in **bold** type in this book, include it in your glossary with a definition and a sample sentence.

SCIENTISTS IN ACTION

Close your eyes for a minute and imagine that you are watching a scientist at work. What does your scientist look like? What is your scientist doing? How do you know that the person you are looking at is a scientist?

Now, open your eyes and draw a picture of your scientist. Compare the drawing you made with a classmate's drawing. How are your drawings the same? How are they different?

All of the people in this picture have to know about science. They use science every day in the work they do. Choose one of the people and make a list in your journal of the kinds of scientific things they need to know about.

INVESTIGATING FURTHER

Changing Gears

Describe what would happen if

- you used 12 toothpicks in gear A and 6 in gear B
- both gears used 12 toothpicks
- a smaller piece of potato was used for gear A

In which direction will the gears turn? How quickly will they turn? Make your predictions and then find out.

Gearing Up

What questions could you ask about gears to help you learn more? Remember, science is all about asking questions and looking for answers to them.

In Getting Started you will examine the gears in a water wheel. In Let's Investigate you will test how large and small gears work together. In Investigating Further you can use a graph to make predictions about gears.

GETTING STARTED

The Greeks and Romans used the moving water of a river to help turn a wheel. The water wheel turned the heavy millstones to grind grain into flour. The flowing water turned the gears, which in turn moved the grinding stones.

Look at the gears in the water wheel. How are they the same? different? What questions could you ask?

LET'S INVESTIGATE

1. Make a small and large gear following the directions in Inside Machines. Put 12 toothpicks around the large gear and 6 around the small gear.

2. Work with a classmate and decide who will turn the gears and who will be the recorder.

3. Make a chart like this in your journal.

Number of Turns	Large Gear	Small Gear

4. Make one turn using the large gear. Record the number of times the small gear turned.

5. Make two and then three turns using the large gear and record the number of turns the small gear makes each time.

6. This time make one, two, and three turns using the small gear. Note any similarities or differences in your journal.

Reflect on Your Results

1. Which gear moved the fastest—the small or the large gear?

2. Which gear moved the slowest?

3. What happened when you changed the gear you turned?

INFORMATION STATION

What Do Gears Do?

Gears can be used to move a force from one place to another. For example, when you pedal a bicycle, you push on the pedals, and gears make the back wheel turn. Gears can also be used to change

the direction of a force. Think of when you made one of your potato gears turn horizontally and it turned the other gear vertically.

When gears of the same size work together they make the same number of turns. When two gears of different sizes work together, however, every time the larger gear turns once, the smaller gear will turn more than once. This means the smaller gear spins faster. Gears of different sizes can be used to change speed.

Gears have been used by scientists since ancient times. Read about one famous scientist in Scientists in Action on the next page.

INVESTIGATING FURTHER

For help making a bar graph, see the Toolkit on page 243.

Using a Graph

Make a bar graph to show how many times the small gear turned when you turned the large gear. Give the graph a title and labels. Compare your graph with a classmate's. Why might there be different results?

Use the graph to predict what will happen if four turns are made. Make a prediction and then check to find out. Add the results to your graph.

SCIENTISTS IN ACTION

Use library books or the Internet to find out about other inventions or discoveries.

Leonardo da Vinci

Leonardo da Vinci was born in 1452 and has been called the first modern scientist. He was also an artist and an inventor. His training as a painter helped him to observe and then draw what he saw. Da Vinci kept a journal with detailed notes of his observations, plans, and experiments.

Da Vinci was fascinated with machines and some of his sketches show how machines worked. Some of the machines he drew already existed and others were inventions of his own. Da Vinci invented many machines that we use today. One of his inventions, the bicycle, was found in one of his notebooks 300 years before it appeared on the road.

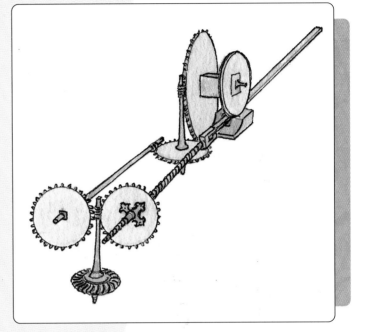

Da Vinci sketched rock formations that he had seen along river banks. In the unit Earth Lab you will learn about different types of rocks.

He tried to make large round mirrors similar to those used today in telescopes. You will use mirrors to investigate light energy in the unit Light Show.

Many of the machines and inventions that we use today began with careful observations. Now it's your turn. Look carefully. Maybe you'll see what others have never seen before.

Pulley Power

How does a crane lift a heavy object? Why do you think cranes rise so high in the air? In Getting Started you will make a simple pulley. In Let's Investigate you will build a model to show how pulleys help us do work.

GETTING STARTED

You, too, can move heavy objects using the same scientific principle used by a crane. Try the following idea to feel the power of this simple machine.

Two classmates stand facing each other, each holding the handle of a broomstick. Tie the end of the rope to one broomstick and loop it around both of the broomsticks a couple of times.

Challenge your classmates to hold the broomsticks apart while you pull on the free end of the rope. What happens?

When the rope is pulled, the broomsticks act as pulleys. Pulleys are another kind of simple machine.

You will need

- a pull-meter (see the Toolkit on page 247)
- 7 large paper clips
- 2 m of string
- a paper cup
- several small objects to use as loads (marbles, interlocking cubes, washers)
- masking tape

You can learn how gears and pulleys are used in other machines in *Eyewitness: Force and Motion* by Peter Lafferty (Stoddart: Toronto, ON, 1992).

Find out how a pulley works.

1. Straighten four paper clips, leaving the hooks at each end. Attach three of them around the rim of the paper cup. Use the fourth paper clip to hook the ends of the three paper clips. Add a load to your cup using a few marbles, interlocking cubes, or washers.

2. Use your pull-meter to lift your cup and load. The elastic band should stretch about 2 to 3 cm. Remove or add to your load until the elastic has stretched that distance.

3. Tie a paper clip to each end of a 10-cm piece of string. Tape one of these paper clips to the edge of a desk so the string and other paper clip are hanging freely over the edge of the desk.

4. Attach another paper clip to one end of a one-metre length of string. Hook your cup and load to this paper clip. Thread the other end through the paper clip hanging from the desk. Lift the load by pulling down on the string attached to the cup.

5. Use your pull-meter to measure how hard you have to pull to lift the load.

6. Try again. This time attach a string to the desk and thread it through the paper clip that holds the cups and load. Use your pull-meter to measure how hard you have to pull to lift the load.

7. Record your observations. Draw pictures and include labels to help describe what you saw.

Reflect on Your Results

1. What did you notice when you pulled on the string? What happened to the load?

2. What are some advantages of using pulleys?

3. Read the Information Station to learn about simple machines that use pulleys.

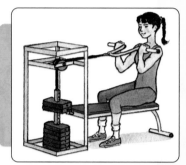

Simple Machines

Gears and pulleys are two examples of simple machines. Simple machines make difficult jobs easier. A **gear** is a wheel with teeth that turns another gear. A **pulley** is usually a wheel that works with a rope or a belt. It is often used to help lift heavy things.

In the first picture, the pulley at the top of the pole helps us pull the flag up when we pull the rope down. This is called a fixed pulley, since the pulley doesn't move.

The second picture also shows a fixed pulley.

Next, a rope and two pulleys are being used to lift a very heavy load. This is sometimes called a block and tackle. The block is just another name for the pulley and the tackle is another name for the rope. One pulley moves and the other one is fixed.

In the picture below, when the line is pulled, the piece of clothing attached to the line moves along.

What Did You Learn?

1. Were the pulleys you made fixed or moving?

2. Which pulleys in the Information Station were yours most like? Why?

Get in Gear

You use gears and pulleys every time you ride your bicycle. Yes, science is everywhere, and you can learn about it by asking questions and looking for answers to your questions.

In Getting Started you will look for pulleys and gears in machines. In Let's Investigate you will examine a simple bicycle and how its gears and pulleys work. In Investigating Further you can examine a bicycle with many gears to see how it works.

GETTING STARTED

Look at this picture. Which machines have gears? Which machines have pulleys?

Look for pulleys and gears around you. Sometimes they are hidden inside larger machines. You may have to ask an adult to help you find them.

You will need
- a bicycle

Try to find the gears on this bicycle. What do you notice about the gears? One gear is attached to the pedal and the other to the rear wheel. What do you notice about the sizes of the two gears? What happens when the pedal is moved?

1. Look carefully at the pedals and back wheel of a bicycle. Count the number of teeth on the gear attached to the pedals.

2. How many teeth are on the gear attached to the rear wheel?

3. While these two gears are not touching, they are connected. What connects the gear on the back wheel to the gear on the pedals?

4. Lift the back wheel off the ground. Slowly, turn the pedals around once. How many turns does the back wheel make? (Don't spin the wheel. Count the turns made by just one turn of the pedals.)

5. Make up a test to see how far your bicycle can travel on one turn of the pedal. Try it.

Keep your fingers a safe distance away from the moving spokes. Move the pedals slowly.

What Did You Learn?

1. Describe how a bicycle moves when you move the pedal.

2. Bicyclists have to stop riding their bikes when the chain falls off. Perhaps this has even happened to you. Why is it impossible to ride a bicycle without a chain?

3. In the 1800s, the pedals on a bicycle were attached to the front wheel. One turn of the pedals meant one turn of the wheel. The front wheel was much bigger than the circle the pedals made. How does the size of the wheel affect the distance you would travel with one turn of the pedals?

INVESTIGATING FURTHER

High Gear, Low Gear

Bicycles have improved since the 1800s. Today's bicycles use several gears to turn the wheels, causing the bicycle to move at different speeds. This makes it possible to ride quickly and climb steep hills.

Look at a bicycle with a number of gears. Watch the gears as they change and see if you can figure out what is happening. Find out which gear makes the wheels turn quickly and which one makes them turn slowly.

SCIENCE ALIVE

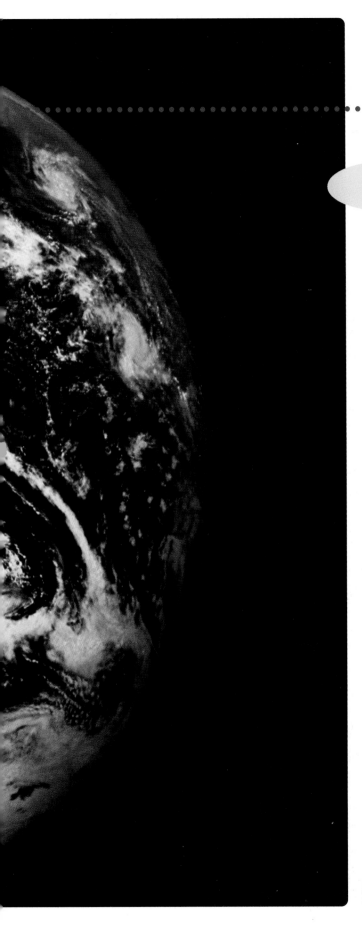

We share this planet with billions of different living things. Each living thing plays an important part in the lives of many others. You already know a lot about living things, but there's always more to discover.

What do you already know about…

1. food linking all living things together?
2. the special features that animals and plants have that help them to survive?
3. how people and the forces of nature affect living things?
4. the danger that living things are in because of us and our actions?

Take a moment to think about these questions. Write your answers in your science journal. Don't worry if you can't think of all the answers right now. Science is always asking questions, looking for answers, and asking new questions. Science is alive!

LIVING SPACES

Our planet has a rich variety of living spaces. There are deserts, forests, meadows, and prairies. There are mountains, boulders, caves, and islands. There are ponds, puddles, rivers, and oceans. You can probably think of many other living spaces.

Look at the photographs above. What plants and animals do you think make these living spaces their home?

In Getting Started you will decide which plants and animals might live in your schoolyard. In Let's Observe you will go out into your schoolyard and see for yourself what plants and animals live there. In Investigating Further you can start your own nature journal.

GETTING STARTED

Your schoolyard is another living space. Which of these animals would you be surprised to see in your schoolyard? Which animals wouldn't surprise you? Why? Which animals do you think live in the schoolyard? Which animals are just visitors?

▲ cat

▲ dog

▲ giraffe

▲ fly

▲ ant

▲ black bear

▲ blue jay

▲ bee

▼ prairie dog

▲ mouse

▲ coyote

▲ frog

▲ ground squirrel

▲ mountain goat

▲ goldfish

▲ moose

▲ duck

▲ deer

▲ baboon

Which of these plants would you be surprised to see in your schoolyard? Which ones wouldn't surprise you? Why?

LET'S OBSERVE

You will need
- your science journal
- a pencil
- something sturdy to write on

So far, you've been exploring your schoolyard using your imagination. Now it's time to go outside.

1. Make a chart like this in your science journal. Use it to record your observations. Give it a title such as "Life in Our Schoolyard."

Life in Our Schoolyard

Living Things I Observed	Where I Observed Them

2. Once you're outside, find a place where you can sit or stand quietly. Don't worry about writing anything just yet. Take two or three minutes to relax and observe your surroundings.

3. Now, in the left column of your chart, record one living thing that you have observed. In the right column, record the living space where you observed it.

4. Continue filling in your chart until your teacher asks you to stop.

5. When you return to class, compare your chart with those of your classmates. Were there any things that you didn't notice? Add these to your chart using a different-coloured pencil.

6. Read the Information Station to find out more about living spaces.

Use as many of your senses as you can when observing your surroundings. Remember to ask yourself questions such as "What do I see?" "What can I hear?" "What do I smell?" "How does it feel?" Remember, it is not safe to taste things unless your teacher tells you that you can.

If you don't know the name of something you observe, make a quick sketch of it and notes about it instead. Be sure to include its shape, size, and any other features you notice.

INFORMATION STATION

Habitat Chat

Scientists have their own special word for a living space. They call it a habitat. A **habitat** is a place where animals, plants, and other living things live.

Habitats can be very large or very small. For example, the world's largest animal, the blue whale, lives in a very large habitat, the ocean. Its habitat stretches from the Arctic to the Equator. Mites are tiny, spider-like animals. They're so small that you need a microscope to see them. Their habitat is also small—this one lives on a flea! What other habitats can you think of?

Smaller habitats can be found within larger habitats. For example, a forest is a large habitat. Inside the forest there might be rotting trees, a pond, shrubs, and different kinds of trees. Each of these things can be a habitat, providing homes for plants, animals, and other living things.

▲ blue whale

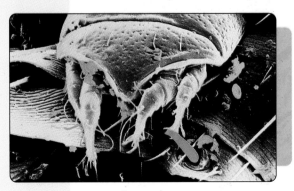

▲ mite

Add the word **habitat** to your science journal. Write its meaning in your own words, and then use it in a sentence.
   Repeat this exercise each time you see a word in **bold** type throughout this unit.

Reflect on Your Results

1. Look at the left column in your chart. How many different living things did you observe? Which ones probably make the schoolyard their full-time home? Which ones do you think are just visitors?

2. Look at the right column in your chart. In how many different living spaces did you find living things?

3. Look at both columns. How many living things did you observe in the same living space?

What Did You Learn?

1. Which of your five senses did you use to make your observations? Which sense did you use the most? Which did you use the least? Why?

2. What surprised you about the number of living things you observed? Explain your answer.

3. How many different living spaces did you observe? Could you call these living spaces habitats? Why or why not?

4. Explain whether or not your whole schoolyard could be called a habitat.

Use library books or the Internet to find out about one of the people listed in Scientists in Action. What living things do or did they like to draw or paint? When and why did they start drawing living things? Where can their work be seen? How do or did they feel about the living things they draw or paint? Include anything else about the artists or their work that interests you. Use your information to draw a poster, or write a short story or magazine article.

INVESTIGATING FURTHER

Start a Nature Journal

Start your own nature journal at home. The next time you're out with your family in a park, at a beach, or in some other natural area, sketch the living things that interest you. If you don't know the names of the plants and animals you see, use a field guide or identification book to help you. What other ways could you find out about the things you observe?

SCIENTISTS IN ACTION

Imagine you are a scientist living a long time ago. You are travelling to a faraway place that no one from your country has ever visited. Your boat lands on shore and you climb out eagerly—after all, you're about to observe marvellous habitats rich with plants and animals that are new to you.

You want to share your discoveries with family and friends back home. You might decide to collect some samples of smaller living things to take back with you. The bigger living things won't fit on your boat, and camcorders and cameras haven't been invented yet. So you decide to draw what you see.

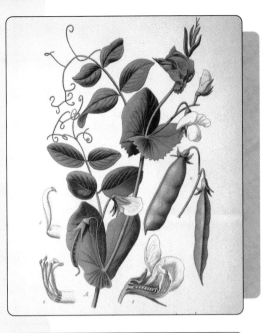

For thousands of years, until photography was invented, scientists and explorers drew pictures in their journals to record their observations. When they returned home, they wrote reports and published books so that others could learn about their amazing discoveries. Many of their sketches and drawings have been preserved in museums and libraries around the world. Some of the most well-known drawings have been created by

- John James Audubon
- Robert Bateman
- Bev Doolittle
- Robert Hooke
- Ely Kish
- Bill Reid

▲ dodo

Even today, many scientists and other lovers of nature use art to record the living things they observe. In some cases they make quick sketches or labelled drawings in their journals to record their observations. In other cases they create full-colour paintings that capture the beauty of living things in their habitats.

FOOD LINKS

What foods do you eat that have nothing to do with plants? Record your answer in your science journal. You'll have a chance to think about the question again later in this learning event.

All living things need food. Food provides energy for plants and animals to live and grow. Food is one of the basic needs for life.

Think about the food you eat. Some of this food comes from plants. Some of it comes from animals. What plant foods do you like to eat? What animal foods do you like to eat? How many of the items in the picture above came from plants? How many came from animals?

In Getting Started you will begin to think about which animals eat plants and which ones eat other animals. In Let's Investigate you will play a game to build food chains. In Investigating Further you can gather information about animals that are scavengers or decomposers.

GETTING STARTED

Picture a small, natural habitat that you have visited, such as a pond, a field, or a forest. Think about an animal that you saw there. Chances are the animal was either looking for something to eat or trying to avoid being eaten.

Make a list of the animals you might see in this habitat. Which of these animals eats other animals? Which ones eat only plants? Which ones eat both? Scientists have a simple way to show how food energy links plants and animals together. It's called a food chain.

INFORMATION STATION

Food Chains: Who's Eating Whom?

All animals need food energy to survive. They get it by eating or consuming other living things. So animals are **consumers.**

All plants need food energy to survive too, but they can do something that animals can't. Plants take energy from the sun and use it to make or produce their own food. So plants are **producers.**

Some animals eat only plants to get the energy they need. They are called **herbivores.** Deer, caterpillars, and chipmunks are examples of herbivores. Other consumers eat only animals and are called carnivores. Lions, wolves, and sharks are examples of **carnivores.** Some consumers eat plants and animals. They are called **omnivores.** Bears, raccoons, and people are examples of omnivores. ▶

Which of these plants and animals are food producers? Which are food consumers? Make two lists. ▼

▲ lynx

maple tree ▲

◀ pond plant (cattails)

▲ tulip

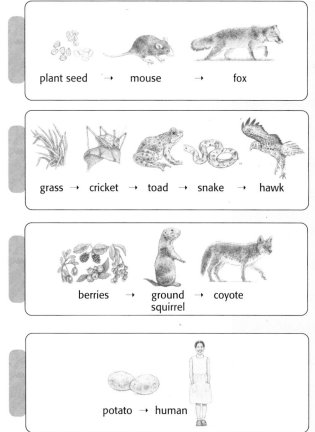

plant seed → mouse → fox

grass → cricket → toad → snake → hawk

berries → ground squirrel → coyote

potato → human

You can show these food relationships in a simple diagram called a **food chain**. A food chain traces the path that food energy travels from producers to consumers. Here are just a few examples of food chains. There are many more in every habitat on our planet.

Food chains can be short, like the potato → human food chain. They can also be long—even longer than the longest example shown here. Long or short, there's something that all food chains have in common. Without it, there wouldn't be any food chains. In fact, there would be no life on earth at all. What do these food chains have in common? See if you can figure out what it is, and why it's so important to all living things.

LET'S INVESTIGATE

Record each food chain you make in your science journal. Put a check mark beside it if it's accepted. Put an "x" beside it if it isn't, and make a quick note to explain why.

This is a game to help you explore food chains. First, be sure you've read the Information Station. Then see how many food chains you can create.

1. Form a group of about four people.

2. Take turns writing the names of 20 plants and 20 animals on a stack of index cards. Write one name on each card. The object of the game is to make food chains using as many cards as you can. Your food chains can be as long or as short as you like.

3. Make sure the cards are well mixed.

4. Deal five cards to everyone in the group. Put the rest of the cards face down in a pile.

5. Each player takes a turn. During your turn, you can choose to do one of the following:

- Show a food chain using some or all of the cards in your hand.
- Draw a new card from the deck.
- Add a card to a completed food chain.
- If you can't use a card you pick, ask each of the other players if they can. If no one can use it, shuffle it back into the pile.

6. When showing a food chain, lay the cards in front of you so everyone can see them. Then explain how the food chain works. The other players in your group decide whether it is a food chain. If they don't think it is a food chain, they must explain why. If the food chain is accepted, the player gets to pick a new card from the remaining cards in the deck. If the food chain isn't accepted, the played-out cards are shuffled back into the deck.

7. The game is over when all available cards have been played or when players can't make any more food chains.

Reflect on Your Results

1. How many food chains did you make?

2. How many of your food chains had two living things in them? How many had three? four? five? more than five?

3. You played the food-chain game with a deck of 40 cards. Twenty cards were plant cards. How would the game be different if you played with only 10 plant cards? How many food chains would you have been able to make if there weren't any plant cards?

Read about what happens when a family of wolves is removed from a food chain in *Wolf Island* by Celia Godkin (Fitzhenry and Whiteside: Toronto, ON, 1993).

What Did You Learn?

1. On page 32, you were asked to think about the foods you eat that have nothing to do with plants. Look at the answer you wrote in your science journal. Give reasons why you now agree or disagree with your answer.

2. Here are some incomplete food chains. Complete each of them at least three different ways. You can make the chains as long or as short as you like.

   ? → spider → ?

   ? → blue whale

   carrots → ?

3. Here's a common food chain in many Canadian habitats.

   grass → mouse → owl

   What might happen in the habitat if there are many owls and few mice? What might happen if there are few owls and many mice? What might happen if there is little grass and many mice? How would this affect the owls?

INVESTIGATING FURTHER

Decomposers and Scavengers

When plants and animals die, their bodies are used as food energy by other groups of consumers. These consumers are called decomposers and scavengers. Use reference sources to find examples of decomposers and scavengers that live in two different habitats. What do they use for food? Do any other living things use them for food? What would happen if the decomposers and scavengers were removed from a habitat? Create two food chains using decomposers and scavengers.

The Hunters and the Hunted

Each of these foxes has special features that help it to survive. One lives in a desert habitat. One lives in an Arctic habitat. One lives in forest and grassland habitats. Which fox do you think lives in which habitat? What clues can help you answer this question? Do you think any of these foxes could switch habitats with each other?

In Getting Started you will discuss how foxes' and lions' adaptations help them to survive. In Let's Investigate you will do an experiment to compare hunting for prey that is easy to see and prey that is hard to see. In Investigating Further you can gather information about animals that migrate.

GETTING STARTED

Animals spend a lot of time searching for food or being hunted. Animals that hunt and eat other animals are called **predators**. The animals that are hunted and eaten by predators are their **prey**.

Prey animals have different body parts and abilities to help protect and hide them from their predators. Not surprisingly, predators have their own body parts and abilities that help them to sneak up on and catch and eat their prey. The body parts and abilities that an animal has to help it survive in its habitat are called **adaptations**.

Look at the pictures of the three foxes on the previous page. They all have different colours of fur. Fur colour is an adaptation that helps foxes blend into their habitat. Why is white fur a useful adaptation for an Arctic habitat?

Here's another adaptation foxes have that helps them survive in their habitat. Foxes don't sweat like you do to remove extra body heat. Instead, they give off heat through their ears. This ability is an adaptation. So are the sizes and shapes of the ears. How might ear size help a desert fox remove extra body heat? How might ear size help keep an Arctic fox from losing too much body heat?

Since food is so important to all living things, animals have developed many adaptations related to food. Think of a lion. What body parts does it have that help it catch and eat food? What abilities help it catch and eat food?

LET'S INVESTIGATE

Skin or fur colour is an adaptation that helps a prey animal hide from predators. It can also help a predator stay hidden or camouflaged when sneaking up on its prey. Some animals' colours blend so well with their habitat that they're hard to see. In this activity, you will be a predator looking for some different-coloured prey. How much prey will you catch? Let's find out!

1. Your teacher will scatter 100 macaroni pieces in an area. These are the prey. Call them "Mackies".

2. Notice that the Mackies are different colours: 25 are yellow, 25 are blue, 25 are brown, and 25 are green.

3. Pretend you and your classmates are a pack of hungry Mackie predators. Your survival depends on finding and catching your prey.

4. You will have five minutes to find and catch as many Mackies as you can. In your science journal, make a chart like this to record the number of Mackies you catch.

5. Wait for your teacher to tell you to start. Then go hunting!

Number of Mackies I Found			
Yellow Mackies	Blue Mackies	Brown Mackies	Green Mackies

Write the names of four animals you know or like in your science journal. List at least three structural adaptations each one has and explain how they help the animal survive in its habitat.

List at least three behavioural adaptations for each animal and explain how they help the animal survive in its habitat.

Reflect on Your Results

1. Which colour of Mackies was easiest to find? Which colour was hardest to find?

2. How did the habitat colour affect your ability to find and catch the Mackies?

3. Green Mackies live in green grass. Suppose only green Mackies will give you food energy. How would that affect your life and the lives of your pack members?

What Did You Learn?

1. How does colour help a prey animal in its habitat? How does it help a predator animal?

2. Pretend you're a prey animal living in the desert. Name three structural adaptations you would like to have and give reasons why you would like to have them.

3. Pretend you're a predator animal living in the forest. Name three behavioural adaptations you would like to have and give reasons why you would like to have them.

INVESTIGATING FURTHER

Animals That Migrate

Another adaptation shared by many animals including some fish and butterflies is the ability to migrate. Read about five animals that migrate. Choose one and prepare a poster that explains

- why it migrates
- where it migrates from
- where it migrates to
- how far it travels
- any adaptations that help it migrate
- any other interesting facts

More About Adaptations

There are many different adaptations that help living things survive in their habitats. Scientists classify them into two main groups: structural and behavioural adaptations.

Structural adaptations are parts of the body that help living things survive in their habitats. Fur is a structural adaptation. Eyes, ears, teeth, paws, legs, tails, and noses are structural adaptations too. What others can you think of?

Behavioural adaptations are the ways in which living things act or behave to help them survive in their habitats. Making a nest is a behavioural adaptation. So is attracting mates, shivering to stay warm, swimming, and hiding. What others can you think of?

Adaptations are the reason living things are found in some habitats and not in others. For example, adaptations let an Arctic fox survive in the Arctic, but they won't help a desert fox live in the same habitat. The Arctic fox's white fur helps to camouflage it in the white snow. The desert fox's brown fur helps it to hide in the desert.

These photos show only three of the 37 members of the cat family. Tigers, jaguars, and your pet cat are three other members. Each member of the cat family has certain structural and behavioural adaptations that help it to survive in its habitat. However, cats share many structural and behavioural adaptations. Which ones can you name?

Some living things are more adaptable than others. They can live in a wide variety of habitats. For example, red foxes are found nearly every-where in Canada.

You know another highly adaptable animal—the most adaptable on the planet. It's you and the rest of your fellow humans!

ADAPTATIONS FOR PLANTS

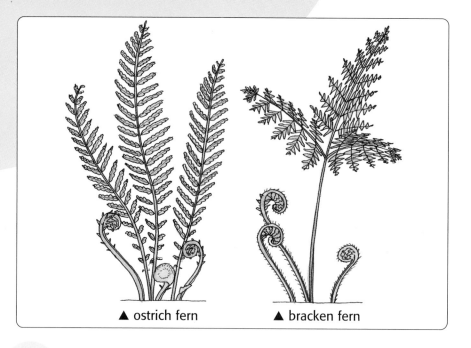

▲ ostrich fern   ▲ bracken fern

You don't want to confuse these two ferns. The young leaves, or fiddleheads, on an ostrich fern are a delicious food. The bracken fern also grows new leaves that look like fiddleheads. However, the fiddleheads of a bracken fern are poisonous.

Fortunately, you won't find these two fern plants growing near one another. Ostrich ferns grow in damp, rich soils. Poisonous bracken ferns prefer drier, open habitats such as fields and pastures.

In **Getting Started** you will match pictures of plants that live in different areas with their descriptions. In **Let's Design** you will design a plant to live in a specific habitat. In **Investigating Further** you can learn how people sometimes control plants' adaptations.

Plant Adaptations

Plants, like animals, have made adaptations for surviving in their habitats. Many kinds of plants share three main adaptations. These are leaves, stems, and roots. These adaptations let plants get the sunlight, water, and nutrients they need.

Plants use sunlight to make the food they need to survive. Leaves are their adaptations for collecting sunlight and making food.

Stems are adaptations that give plants support so they can stand up. Leaves grow out of stems. The stems serve as "pipelines", carrying water and nutrients to the leaves and food to the rest of the plant.

Roots are adaptations that help hold the plants in place. The roots collect water and nutrients from the soil, and send them to the stems and the leaves.

GETTING STARTED

Leaves, stems, and roots let plants survive in nearly every habitat on earth. However, different habitats receive different amounts of sunlight, water, and soil nutrients. Look at these pictures and descriptions to find out how these plants have adapted. See if you can match each picture with its description on the next page.

Pitcher Plant

This plant grows in marshy, swampy habitats where the soil is low in nutrients. Its leaves are shaped like funnels and allow the plant to collect rainwater. The insides of the leaves are slippery, and the plant produces a sweet juice that attracts insects. When the insects land, they slip and drown in the collected water at the bottom of the leaves. The plant then digests the insects to obtain their nutrients.

Saguaro Cactus

The saguaro cactus grows in very hot and dry habitats. It has a thick, spongy stem to hold water. The stem also has a waxy coating to keep water from escaping. The plant's roots are very long, grow close to the ground's surface, and extend from the plant in all directions. This root system helps the plant collect as much as possible of the small amount of rain that falls.

Dwarf Willow

The dwarf willow grows in habitats where there are strong winds, little rainfall, and very cold temperatures much of the year. Its stem grows very low to the ground, where the effects of the icy wind are less severe. During the long, cold winters, this plant is often completely covered by snow, which protects it from the wind.

Orchid

This plant grows in moist, damp habitats. Unlike most plants, this one prefers to grow on trees. The orchid's roots cling to tree trunks and branches, taking in water and nutrients from the tree and moist air.

LET'S DESIGN

Design and build a plant that can live in a specific habitat.

1. Choose one of these designs. Design a plant that
   - can live in a watery habitat
   - is safe from lawnmowers
   - is safe from cows and other livestock
   - can live without water for long periods of time
   - can live in very cold temperatures for long periods of time
   - can grow on apartment balconies that receive very little sunlight

2. Draw a plan of your plant before you begin. Use labels to show your plant's adaptations and how these adaptations help it survive in its habitat.

3. When you're satisfied with your plan, go ahead and build your plant.

Reflect on Your Results

1. What do plants need to survive?
2. Describe the habitat in which your invented plant lives.
3. List all the adaptations you gave your invented plant.
4. Explain how your plant's adaptations help it get what it needs to live.

You will need
- a pencil and paper
- recycled materials such as yarn, string, buttons, pipe cleaners or soft wire, paper, cardboard, plastic foam trays, elastic bands
- tape or glue
- crayons or paints

While you build your plant, you may come up with new ideas for adaptations you want to give it. That's great! Make notes of any changes on your plan.

Leaves, stems, and roots all work together for the same purpose. In your science journal, explain the purpose of these three adaptations.

Most plants make more of their kind, or reproduce, by making seeds. Plant seeds have an amazing variety of adaptations. Look for seed adaptations in your neighbourhood. (If it's the wrong time of year, you'll have to do your hunting in the library or on the Internet.) See how many different seed adaptations you can find. Be sure to explain in your science journal how each of them works.

What Did You Learn?

1. Name three adaptations that help plants get what they need to live. How does each of these adaptations help the plant survive?

2. Are there any adaptations you wish you had given your plant? Are there any you wish you hadn't? Revise your plan. Include labels to describe your plant's new adaptations. Then write a short paragraph comparing your original plan with your new one. Be sure to describe any changes you made and explain why you made them.

3. Name any habitats on earth you can think of where plants can't grow. Why can't they grow there?

4. Read Scientists in Action. Why do you think the trees would get smaller and more scattered as the scientists travelled farther north? What do you think "finally disappearing altogether" means?

5. Why do you think the soil in the Arctic would have very few nutrients? What does that tell you about the root adaptations of Arctic plants?

INVESTIGATING FURTHER

For some help with gathering information, read page 248 of the Toolkit.

Changing the Way Plants Adapt
Scientists have learned enough about plants that they can change some plants' adaptations. Find out how and why wheat, tomato, and potato adaptations were changed by scientists.

SCIENTISTS IN ACTION

Two Canadian scientists, Lynn Gillespie and Laurie Consaul, visited the Arctic in August 1997. They were there to gather data, collect samples, and take photos for an interactive computer guide to Canadian Arctic plants. They were also studying how plants have adapted to life in the Arctic. While they were there, they did what all good scientists do. They made journal notes to record what they observed and what they did. Here are some highlights from their journal notes.

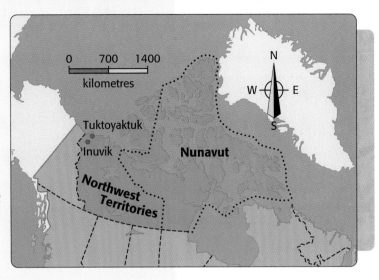

August 4: Our 12-seater plane from Inuvik to Tuktoyaktuk (Tuk for short) followed the eastern edge of the Mackenzie Delta. On our left, waterways, islands, and lagoons stretched as far as the eye could see. The two-metre- to four-metre-high spruce trees that we saw around Inuvik gradually became smaller and more scattered, finally disappearing altogether.

August 7: Our camp was on a giant berry patch. We were surrounded by blueberries, crowberries, bearberries, mountain cranberries, and cloudberries. It is impossible not to step on the low, ground-hugging shrubs laden with ripe fruit.... We went on a long hike across the Arctic landscape along the Delta, exploring the many habitats, with a watchful eye for grasses.

August 9: The area around our camp was carpeted in tiny flowers: purple gentians, white and yellow seaside daisies, mauve Arctic fleabane, white anemones, and pink seathrift. Even the willow tree lay flat on the ground, barely five centimetres high, evidence of the strong winds that often sweep across the Cape. Only the grasses, scattered here and there, rose above this colourful carpet.

August 14: Arctic soils have very few nutrients. Our search among the dunes yielded some blue grass with seed, our first collection of seed on this trip. The summer growing season is so short here that plants often do not make seeds every year.

Courtesy Canadian Museum of Nature condensed from their Website <www.nature.ca/english/field-lg.htm>.

How Many Are There?

Name the three different habitats pictured here. How many living things are there in each of the pictures? How many more might there be in the world? Why would scientists want to know? How could they find out?

When you were making observations of life in your schoolyard you listed the living things you saw. The number of living things in a habitat makes up a population. For example, let's say you noticed there were four maple trees living in your schoolyard. That means your schoolyard has a population of four maple trees.

In some cases, many different populations share the same habitat. Other habitats only support a few different populations. All of the populations living in the same habitat make up a community.

In **Getting Started** you will practise counting a small number of things to estimate a large number. In **Let's Experiment** you will use what you have learned to estimate the plant populations in your schoolyard.

GETTING STARTED

Counting the members in a population is a challenge. Imagine trying to count all the grass plants in a park or all the birch trees in a forest. As difficult as this can be, at least plants stay still. Animals are almost always on the move. Imagine how challenging it is to figure out animal populations!

Fortunately, scientists have invented several ways to solve this problem. One way is to count each living thing one by one. This only works for small populations. What about large populations? Counting one by one would take a very long time.

Most of the techniques involve estimating the size of a population. When you estimate, you find out approximately how many things there are by using a number you already know.

For example, about how many letter *e*'s are there on this page?

Take the "Eeeeek!" Challenge: What is the population of letter *e*'s on this page?

You will need
- a piece of cardboard (or sticky note)
- a calculator
- a textbook

1. Cut a square of cardboard that is 5 cm long and 5 cm wide. You could also use a sticky note. Place it over the text at the upper right of the page.

2. Count the letter *e*'s that are inside the square. If the edges of the square touch any letter *e*'s, count them, too. Record the number. You have just taken a sample of the letter *e*'s found on this page.

3. Estimate the number of squares that would fit on the page. Then multiply the number of squares by the number of *e*'s in your sample. You can use your calculator if you wish.

4. This is your estimate for the number of *e*'s on the page.

5. You can check your results. How? By counting each *e* one by one. Compare both numbers to see how close your estimate was to the actual total.

LET'S EXPERIMENT

You will need
- four craft sticks
- about 5m of string
- a metre stick or measuring tape

In this group activity you will use the estimating method you just learned to find the plant populations in your schoolyard habitat. There are two parts to this activity. In the first part, you'll focus on one small area of the schoolyard. In the second part, you'll think about how to use what you have learned to count all the plants in the schoolyard!

PART 1: COUNTING PLANT POPULATIONS IN A SQUARE METRE

If you don't know the name of any plant you observe, describe it instead. Use words, a sketch, or both to record your description.

1. Choose a part of the schoolyard to do your sampling. Make a square on the ground that measures 1 m long and 1 m wide. Use the craft sticks as corners for the square. Attach the string to the sticks to mark the four sides.

2. Make a chart like this in your science journal. Use it to record your observations.

Plant Populations	
Kind of Plant We Observed	How Many We Counted

3. Use your chart to help you list and count the different plants in your area. Decide how your group wants to organize the work. For example, one group member can start in each corner and work his or her way toward the centre. If your group does this, each person will make a separate chart. You can combine the results later.

4. When you're finished doing your population counts, answer the Reflect on Your Results questions.

Reflect on Your Results

1. How many populations did you observe in your area?

2. Which kind of plant in your sample has the largest population?

3. Which has the smallest population?

4. Explain why you think the results are or are not the same for the whole schoolyard. What could you do to find out if they are true?

PART 2: HOW MANY PLANT POPULATIONS ARE THERE IN YOUR SCHOOLYARD?

In this part of the activity, you'll be finding the populations of all the plants in your schoolyard. There aren't any instructions though. It's up to you and your classmates to decide how to do it. As a class, develop a plan. Your teacher will help if you need it. When you're ready, put your plan into action!

Reflect on Your Results

1. Which of these statements best describes how you got your population results?
   - We counted each type of plant in the schoolyard one by one.
   - We estimated the number of each type of plant found in the schoolyard.
   - We took a sample by counting the number of plants in a small area. We estimated the number of samples in the schoolyard and then multiplied the two numbers together for our final estimate.

2. How accurate do you think your population numbers are? Why do you think so?

3. If you were going to do part 2 of this activity again, what would you do differently?

Make a list in your science journal of four animal populations and four plant populations that you would expect to see in a pond community. Make similar lists for a grassland and a rain-forest community.

What Did You Learn?

1. Explain the advantages and disadvantages of counting one by one.

2. How does finding a sample help when estimating?

3. Scientists often use math skills as a tool to help in their studies. In what ways is math a helpful tool in this activity?

SCIENCE IN OUR LIVES

What would it be like if you made a discovery that caught the attention of scientists and reporters from around the world? This is what happened in 1995 to a class of students only a few years older than you are.

Their class was on a field trip to a local wetlands habitat in Minnesota. The students noticed that some of the members of the frog population looked "weird". They quickly realized that the frogs were much more than weird. They were seriously deformed.

Some frogs had extra legs and other body parts. Some had deformed eyes. Some were missing body parts. The students made notes in their science journals. They found that about half of the frog population they sampled that day had deformities.

Within a year of the discovery, there were reports of more frog deformities from all over the state of Minnesota. At the same time, similar findings were being made in other states, in Canada, and in other countries around the world. Scientists were now concerned.

Frogs are important predators of insects and other small creatures. They are also prey for many different kinds of predators. Sick frogs pose a threat to the survival of many other living things.

The health of frogs reflects the health of our habitat on earth. That's because frogs, like all amphibians, live in water as well as on land. They can be affected by harmful pollutants in both habitats. Scientists had seen cases of frog deformities, but these were usually in habitats near our towns and cities, where pollution could be the cause. Now shockingly high numbers of sick frogs are turning up in habitats that scientists thought were safe.

When large numbers of frogs start to become unhealthy and die, it's a warning to us that other living things—including humans— may be in danger.

Scientists are still looking for answers to the frog-deformity problem. Meanwhile, an organization in Minnesota called the Center for Global Environmental Education has set up a program called "A Thousand Friends of Frogs". This program links together students, teachers, and other concerned people by asking them to do frog surveys in local wetlands. This way, everyone works together to find out where there are normal frog populations and where there are abnormal frog populations. Would you like to become another friend of frogs? Use the Internet to find out the latest information about this group.

HABITATS CHANGE

Habitats are constantly changing. Some of these changes are very slow. Others are very fast. Some are caused by natural forces. Others are caused by humans. Look at these photographs. Decide how the changes were made—by nature or by humans. How do you think the changes to these habitats affect living things?

In Getting Started you will imagine how your life would change if you moved to another country. In Let's Investigate you will read a case study about some reindeer that were moved.

GETTING STARTED

In a small group choose a country that you think is very different from Canada. Imagine that you and your family moved there. What parts of life might be easier in that country? Why? What might you find more difficult? Why? Discuss your answers in your group.

LET'S INVESTIGATE

Imagine you're a prey animal living in a habitat without predators and with a lot of food. What would happen to the habitat? Read this case study and answer the questions to find out.

CASE STUDY: WHAT HAPPENED TO THE REINDEER ON ST. MATTHEW ISLAND?

In 1944, a small population of reindeer was moved from their Arctic habitat on Nunivak Island to a similar habitat on St. Matthew Island. At that time the total population of the reindeer herd was 29.

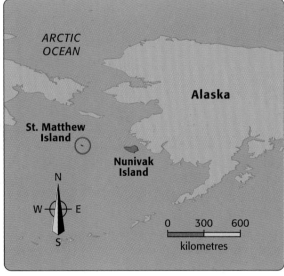

For the reindeer, St. Matthew Island might have been a dream come true. Only a few other animals were adapted for life on the island. These were mainly voles (rodents related to rats and mice) and Arctic foxes. Neither of these is a predator of reindeer.

There was plenty of food, including low-growing Arctic grasses and Arctic willows. In particular, there were plenty of plant-like living things called lichens. The lichen population was so large that it limited the number of grasses and willows that could grow and survive. At first this was not a problem for the reindeer. Lichens are their favourite winter food and the main source of their food energy during the long winter.

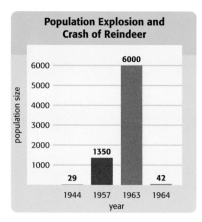

Population Explosion and Crash of Reindeer

The next time people visited the island was in 1957. They set out on foot to count the reindeer population, one by one. The population at that time was 1350 reindeer. Scientists also sampled the plant populations to see what the reindeer were eating and where. They used a square-metre area, just like you did on page 51, to estimate the total number of plants. It turned out that the reindeer were getting most of their food in two areas in the southeast part of the island. That was where the lichen population was the largest. There were also signs at that time that the lichen supply was beginning to shrink.

Six years later, scientists visited the island once again. The scientists surveyed the island using a helicopter. The reindeer population now stood at 6000!

Unfortunately, the lichen population was now almost completely gone. Most of it had been eaten by the reindeer. Much of the rest had been heavily trampled. Very few lichens still survived, and it would take years for them to grow and increase their numbers.

With so little winter food remaining, the stage was set for a disaster. Severe cold and heavy snowfalls during the winter of 1963 to 1964 made it hard for the huge reindeer population to find the already short supply of food. When scientists visited the island in the spring of 1964, they discovered vast numbers of dead reindeer. Nearly the whole population had died. There were only 42 survivors.

Reindeer are large members of the deer family. They are close cousins of the caribou. Their large, wide hoofs and heavy, thick fur are two adaptations that help them to survive in Arctic habitats. ▶

Reflect on Your Results

1. How did the reindeer population change their habitat? How did the changed habitat affect the reindeer? How do you think the changed habitat affected the voles and the Arctic foxes? Explain your answer.

2. How would you describe the habitat changes that took place on St. Matthew Island? Were they caused by natural forces or by human activities?

What Did You Learn?

1. In the case study, what two methods did the scientists use to figure out populations? Which method do you think gave them more accurate information? Why?

2. How do you know that the St. Matthew Island reindeer had adaptations that suited them for living in their new habitat?

3. Reindeer live in Arctic habitats around the world. When the reindeer run out of food or if there is poor weather, they move or migrate to other, more suitable habitats. Why didn't the St. Matthew Island reindeer do this?

4. Name an animal and a plant that change their habitats. Explain how the habitat changes in each case.

5. How do you and your family affect your habitat?

6. How do other people in the world affect habitats?

LIVING THINGS IN DANGER

When a habitat changes, the plants and animals that live there can find it difficult to survive.

In **Getting Started** you will examine a human community and a pond community. In **Let's Investigate** you will gather information about Canadian animals and plants that are in danger. In **Investigating Further** you can research groups of people that help animals and plants in danger.

GETTING STARTED

Look at the two communities on page 58. One is a human community and the other a pond community.

What different populations can you see in the pond community? What other populations might also live there?

What populations of living things make their home in the human community? Has anyone from the human community visited the pond community? How do you know? Has anything from the pond community visited the human community? Explain.

LET'S INVESTIGATE

All over the world there are populations whose numbers are so low that they are in danger of disappearing from our planet forever. When that happens, they are said to be extinct. Here are just a few Canadian plants and animals that are in danger.

People often use terms such as "extinct" and "endangered" to talk about animals that are in danger because of us. Scientists use these terms, too. Scientists use them to classify living things based on the amount of danger their populations face in the wild. They also use terms such as "critically endangered" and "threatened". Write these four "in danger" terms in your science journal. Then put them in an order that makes sense to you. Compare your order with the order some of your classmates chose.

Some Canadian Plants That Are in Danger

- American ginseng
- golden seal
- jacob's ladder
- phantom orchid
- swamp rose mallow

Some Canadian Animals That Are in Danger

- barn owl
- blue whale
- eastern massasauga rattlesnake
- grey fox
- long-billed curlew
- peary caribou
- spotted bat
- spotted turtle
- trumpeter swan
- white-headed woodpecker
- wood bison

1. Choose one of these living things to investigate. If there's another threatened Canadian plant or animal that interests you, talk to your teacher about choosing it instead.

2. Use the following questions to help guide you in your investigation:
   - What do I already know about this plant or animal?
   - How can I find out more? (Where can you search for information?)
   - What does it look like? What is its habitat?
   - What adaptations does my plant or animal have that suit it for its habitat?
   - How have people changed this habitat to put this living thing in danger?
   - What actions, if any, are people taking to help protect my plant or animal and its habitat?

3. When you have finished your research, write a report to record your findings.

Reflect on Your Results

1. What did you find out about your plant or animal that you didn't know? Does anything you learned surprise you? Explain your answer.

2. What type of research did you do? Are there any other information sources that you might have used? Talk this over with some of your classmates to see how they did their research.

3. Are there other plants or animals in danger that share the same habitat as the one you chose? If so, list them. Check to see if any of your classmates investigated them.

Read about the lifestyles of and folklore about jaguars, whooping cranes, wolves, and many other fascinating animals in **The Untamed World series** (Weigl Educational Publishers: Calgary, AB, 1996).

What Did You Learn?

1. When people move into or take over the habitats of other living things, what do they use the habitats for? List at least five examples.

2. Do you agree that habitat changes pose very little threat to living things? Use two examples to help explain why you agree or disagree.

3. Why do you think people are concerned about protecting plants and animals that are in danger? Give reasons for your answers.

Habitat Connections

▲ What would it be like to live in an Arctic habitat or in the mountains? What clothes would you wear? What food would you eat? Where would you get your water?

All living things have an impact on their habitat. You saw this with the reindeer on St. Matthew Island in the previous learning event. They ate so many lichens that the lichen population became smaller and smaller. This had an impact on the reindeer themselves. With so little food left, most of them starved to death.

The reindeer had another impact on the island. (This wasn't included in the case study.) With nearly all the lichens gone, other plant populations—mainly grasses—were able to grow in areas where lichens used to be. Before that, there were so many lichens that they prevented other plants from growing.

What does all this mean? It means that all living things are connected with one another and their habitats. Changes are felt by everything in the habitat. It doesn't matter if the changes are big or small. However, if the changes are big enough, many populations feel the effects of them.

That brings us to humans. People. Us!

We can do something that very few living things can do. We can live in nearly every habitat on the planet. That's because we are able to solve problems, using our knowledge to make any habitat suit our needs. Because we can grow our own food, we usually don't have the same food-shortage problems that the reindeer on St. Matthew Island did. So, like the reindeer, our population has increased dramatically. As the number of people grows we need lots of living space. We usually get it by moving into and taking over the living spaces of other living things. These changes affect the other living things. In this learning event you have begun to find out how.

INVESTIGATING FURTHER

Who Is Helping?

Scientists estimate there could be as many as 100 000 lions in the wilds of Africa. With populations this large, African lions should be around for many years to come. However, there's a single population of about 200 lions in Asia that is a different story. Do some exploring to find out about the Asiatic lion and why it is considered endangered.

Many people around the world try to save plants and animals that are seriously in danger of becoming extinct. Some of these people work mainly by themselves or with small groups of dedicated volunteers. Others work in large organizations. What examples of people and organizations can you find? If you were going to volunteer to help, which person or organization would you choose? Why?

HABITAT SURVIVAL GUIDE

Do you remember the questions you thought about at the start of this unit? Return to page 25. Answer the questions again. Then turn to the science journal page where you recorded your earlier answers. What new things have you learned? What new questions do you have about living things and their habitats?

In **Getting Started** you will discuss changes to habitats. In **Let's Design** you will design a habitat for living things. In **Investigating Further** you can develop a plan to help living things and their habitats.

GETTING STARTED

It has been a mild winter again, for the third year in a row. Spring has brought plenty of sunshine and rain, so the plant life is rich, lush, and green. Last year, people had noticed that there were lots of deer in the area. This year, the deer population is even bigger. Many people enjoy seeing deer in the heart of their city. Unfortunately, some of the deer have wandered onto the streets and have nearly caused accidents. Why do you think there might be so many deer? What do you think will happen next?

A family has moved into a new home that backs onto a farmer's field. On the first night, they hear scratching and noises coming from the basement. Mice! Why might mice be coming into their home? What do you think will happen next?

A neighbourhood park has been plagued with weeds. The town council decides to have the grass sprayed with a herbicide—a poison to kill the weeds. After two weeks, many of the weeds have died. However, people visiting the park have noticed some birds lying dead in the grass. Why might this be happening? What do you think will happen next?

The materials and equipment you will need will depend on what your design plans are. Here are some suggestions:

- cardboard boxes
- modelling clay
- scrap wood pieces or craft sticks
- cotton batting
- sand
- scrap paper
- paints
- plastic or homemade figurines of plants and animals

You've learned a lot about plants and animals and how they are adapted for life in their habitats. If you were going to design the perfect natural habitat for living things, what would it be like?

1. You will be designing a habitat display. All the things you have learned in this unit will help you. Start by choosing a habitat that interests you. Will it be a forest, a grassland, a pond, an Arctic habitat, or something else? Will it be a Canadian habitat or one in another part of the world?

2. Start by sketching your design ideas on paper. These questions will also help you get started.

   Some Habitat Idea Questions
   - What living things do you want to include models of? What part will they play in the habitat?
   - What do these living things need to survive? How can you make sure your habitat provides these things?
   - What landforms would be good for your habitat?
   - How big do you want to make the populations?

   Some Habitat Construction Questions
   - How big do you want to make your habitat? Big enough to fit on a desk or a table?
   - Can your habitat be moved easily?
   - What materials do you need to build your habitat? Do you need any tools to help you put it together?
   - How will you include living things in your model? Will you make them? Will you use plastic figurines you have at home? Will you cut out pictures?

3. When you're satisfied with your plans, show them to your teacher. Then get started. Your habitat awaits you!

Reflect on Your Results

1. What living things did you include in your habitat? How many are producers? How many are consumers?

2. Identify all the prey animals and predator animals in your habitat. Do any of the predators like the same kind of prey? Will that cause problems in the future?

3. List at least three food chains that exist in your habitat. List more if you can.

4. How large are the populations in your habitat? Will any of them get too big? Will any of them get too small? How do you know?

5. Create a Habitat Guidebook, so people who visit your habitat will know what fascinating things there are to explore. Your Habitat Guidebook could have nature trails for people to follow. What else could it have?

What Did You Learn?

1. Visit the habitats your classmates designed. How do they compare with yours? What producers and consumers can you identify? What predators and prey can you name? What food chains do you recognize? How large are the populations?

2. Pretend that your own perfect habitat really exists. What will it look like 10 years from now? How will the landscape be different? How will the kinds and numbers of living things have changed?

3. What events (natural or human-related) might put the plants in your habitat in danger? What about the animals?

4. Read Scientists in Action to find out about some people who help provide safe habitats for animals that are in danger, or neglected or abused by uncaring humans.

SCIENTISTS IN ACTION

Link Up with Rescued Wildlife

All over the world, people are caring for wild animals that have been taken from their native habitats and forced to live in new ones. Even though many of these animals are adapted for life in a variety of habitats, they are not adapted for life among humans.

Unfortunately, baby animals such as lion cubs, chimps, and piglets are cute—so cute that people think that they can share their lives with them. Usually, when the animals get bigger, they become too hard to deal with. They often end up living miserable, unhealthy lives unless they are rescued.

Fortunately, many people have come to the animals' aid. Many organizations all over the world help to rescue and protect endangered plants and animals. One of these groups, the Living Prairie Museum, is in Winnipeg, Manitoba. It is a 12-hectare preserve that is home to prairie plants and wildlife. The tall prairie grass that used to cover about one-million square kilometres in central North America is now almost gone. The Living Prairie Museum saves this disappearing habitat.

Another organization saves and protects members of the cat family. The Cat Tales Endangered Species Conservation Park was founded in 1991. Seven years later it was home to more than 24 big cats. The park has also rescued leopards, tigers, pumas, and bobcats.

The Earth Sanctuaries Ltd. wildlife preserve began in 1988 in Australia. Australia is losing its wildlife faster than any other country. Through the preserve's efforts, 12 species of endangered animals have increased their populations.

INVESTIGATING FURTHER

How Can I Help?

Is there anything that you and your friends can do, personally, to help living things and their habitats? Brainstorm a list, and select something that you'd like to do. Develop an action plan. Then go for it. Make a difference!

THINKING ABOUT SCIENCE ALIVE

1. Draw and label a picture of a food chain. Name the producers and the consumers.

2. Describe the habitat of the plant below.

3. How do you know it gets what it needs to live?

4. Explain how a polar bear has adapted to its Arctic habitat.

5. Describe the habitat of the plant below.

6. How has it adapted to get what it needs to survive?

Soundscapes

Our five senses—sight, hearing, touch, smell, and taste—give us a lot of information about our surroundings. Smell and taste are related. Sometimes, when you smell something you really like, you can almost taste it. Which sense is hearing related to?

Sound is everywhere. What do you already know about...

1. how sound travels?
2. how you hear sounds?
3. what makes sounds loud or soft?
4. what makes sounds high or low?
5. how you can keep unwanted sounds out of your life?

What else would you like to discover about sound?

Write your answers to these questions in your science journal. If you can't think of some answers right now, don't worry. When you finish your study of sound, look back at your answers. See how much you've learned.

Surrounded by Soundscapes

Wherever you go, you are surrounded by sound. In Getting Started you will think about where you might hear certain sounds. In Let's Observe you will list the sounds you might hear in different places. In Investigating Further you can start a collection of sounds.

GETTING STARTED

Where might you hear one of these sounds? Try to think of as many places as possible.

Draw a large square or rectangle in your science journal, and then draw the places in the square. Compare your sound pictures with those of your classmates. How many different places did your class think of to draw?

LET'S OBSERVE

What kinds of sounds can you hear? How are they similar? "Look" for some sounds to find out.

1. Draw a chart like the one below in your science journal.

Sounds I Would Hear in Each Picture	
Place	Sounds
intersection	

You can either write the name of the sound or a description of the sound.

2. Look at the scenes in these photos. Imagine what sounds you would hear if you were standing in each place. List as many sounds as you can for each place on your chart.

What Did You Learn?

1. Choose two of the sounds you listed for each picture (a total of six sounds). For each sound, answer these questions:
   - What is making the sound? (What is the source of the sound?)
   - How is the sound being made?
   - Is it a sound you would like to hear? Why or why not?
2. Look at all the sounds you listed in your chart. In what ways are the sounds different? In what ways might they be similar?
3. This unit is called "Soundscapes". What do you think a soundscape is? List or describe as many soundscapes as you can think of.

INVESTIGATING FURTHER

Collecting Sounds

Start a sound collection. You could record sounds with a tape recorder, or you could draw pictures of what makes the sounds. Choose sounds that you can hear mainly in one place and not in any others. Then, challenge your classmates to name each sound, guess where it was recorded or where they might hear it, and tell you how it's made.

Sound in Motion

You may have heard this riddle: "If a tree falls in a forest and there's no one there to hear it, does it make a sound?" You may have heard this one, too: "What is the sound of one hand clapping?"

These riddles can be answered in different ways. How do you think a scientist would answer them? How would you answer them?

In Getting Started you will decide how you think sounds are made. In Let's Experiment you will make sounds using different materials and try to identify the sounds that others in your class make with different materials. In Investigating Further you can learn how sound effects are made.

GETTING STARTED

What do you think sounds are? How are they made?

Work with a partner to come up with an experiment a scientist could do to learn how sound is made. Then, share your idea with your class.

LET'S EXPERIMENT

You have probably heard your teacher ask the class to talk more quietly or to keep the noise down. Now's your chance to make noise that your teacher actually wants you to make! The catch is that you will have to think about the sounds you make and the way you are making them.

You will need
- aluminum foil
- bags (plastic and paper)
- combs
- balloons
- beans (dried)
- stiff brushes
- small cardboard boxes
- small plastic and wood containers
- cutlery (metal and plastic)
- metal cans
- old toothbrushes
- wooden spoons
- paper (different kinds)

Don't forget to fill in your chart each time you create a sound.

1. Team up with a classmate. Decide who will be the first sound maker and who will be the first sound observer.

2. Make a chart like this in your science journal.

Making Sounds		
What I Made the Sound With	How I Made the Sound	Name of Sound
a balloon		

3. Let the sound maker choose five items from the materials collected for this activity.

4. Position yourselves so that the sound observer faces away from the sound maker.

5. As the sound maker, make a sound using one or more of the items you chose. Can the sound observer name the item you used to make the sound with and what the sound was?

6. Make as many different sounds as you can (your teacher will tell you when to switch roles).

7. Return your items to the collection, and let the new sound maker choose five items from it. Repeat steps 4 to 6.

1. How successful were you in identifying the objects that were used to make the sounds? What clues helped you? Which objects, if any, were difficult to identify? Explain why.

2. Look at your chart and your classmate's chart. Make a list of all the words you both used to describe how the sounds were made. For example, you might both have the words "rubbing" and "banging" in your charts. What other words describe how sounds are made?

3. In what ways are your sound-making words different? In what ways are they the same?

4. What do you notice that all sound making has in common?

5. With your partner's help, choose the best way to complete the following sentence: "Sounds are created when…"

INFORMATION STATION

What Is Sound?

When something moves, it creates vibrations—which in turn can create sound. The kind of movement doesn't matter. It can be a hummingbird's wings flapping so fast you can hardly see them. It can be a drumstick pounding on a drum so hard you can hear it down the street. It can be the wind blowing so gently you can barely see the leaves rustling.

Scientists describe a **vibration** as a back-and-forth movement. Vibrations can be faster than a mosquito's wings. Vibrations can also be slower than a hummingbird's wings.

Although sounds are vibrations, that doesn't mean we can hear all vibrations! What kinds of vibrations might you not be able to hear? If you don't know, don't worry. You'll find out about this later in the unit.

Add the word **vibration** to your science journal. Write its meaning in your own words, and then use it in a sentence. Do this each time you see a word in **bold** type throughout this unit.

What Did You Learn?

1. Write a definition for sound as a scientist might write it. Include three examples to help others better understand the definition.

2. Name different ways you could use a rock, a piece of paper, and a pencil to create sounds. What do the sounds have in common? How many different sounds could you create?

3. In the introduction to this learning event, you thought about two riddles. What were your answers to them? What are your answers now? Have your answers changed? If so, why?

INVESTIGATING FURTHER

Sound Effects

Sound-effects experts work with sound every day. What kinds of tools do they use in their work? See how many different ways to create sound effects you can find out about.

Ancient Vibrations—Drums

The sound of drums has been vibrating around the world for thousands of years. Drums have probably been in existence for as long as there have been humans on the planet. Most cultures have invented their own type of this ancient musical instrument.

We use the sound of drums to create music, of course. However, drums are also important for sending signals over long distances and in religious and spiritual ceremonies.

Why has the drum been invented so many times by so many different people in so many different places? Perhaps the vibrations drums create remind us of heartbeats. Can you think of any other reasons?

▲ How many of these drums have you ever seen? Do you know of any other types of drums?

Sound Travel

Many TV shows and movies are about spaceships and space travel. In them we often hear sound effects for the sound of the engines powering up and for the whoosh as the ship streaks away.

Although many scientists like watching these shows, they know that these sound effects are not scientifically correct. Why?

In Getting Started you will explain what you already know about how sound travels. In Let's Experiment you will explore many ways that sound can travel. In Investigating Further you can gather information about how quickly sound travels.

GETTING STARTED

Think about this question: "Does sound travel in air?" What proof could you use to help you convince someone that it does? Write your answer in your science journal.

LET'S EXPERIMENT

Perhaps you've wondered how sound travels and how we hear sounds. Maybe you've asked yourself or your teacher questions like these:

- **How does sound travel from its source to me?**
- **Does sound travel through air?**
- **What else might sound travel through?**
- **Does sound travel better in some things than in others?**

Here's your chance to explore these questions.

PART 1: SCRATCHING FOR SOUND

1. Stand about a metre apart from a classmate. Hold the broom handle upright. Scratch the top of it with your fingernail while your partner listens with eyes closed. Scratch it gently and then hard. Which sound is easier to hear? Record your observations in your science journal.

2. Hold the broom handle horizontally so that one end touches your partner's ear. Ask your partner to help by supporting the broom handle with one hand.

3. Gently scratch the top end of the handle with your fingernail while your partner listens with eyes closed.

4. Change places with your partner, and repeat steps 1 to 3. What did you hear? Record your observations.

You will need

- for Part 1: a broom handle or metre stick
- for Part 3: a piece of string 3 m long, 2 cups (paper or foam), and a nail
- for Part 4: an aquarium or large glass bowl and 2 small rocks
- for Part 5: whatever materials you choose

Ears are very delicate, so they're easy to damage. Be careful when you hold anything in or near an ear.

Reflect on Your Results

1. In step 1, what proof do you have that the scratching sound travelled through the air?

2. In step 3, did the scratching sound travel through the broom handle? What proof do you have that it did?

3. Did you notice anything else about the scratching sound in steps 1 and 3?

PART 2: MARCH ON!

1. Stand about 2 m away from your partner. March on the spot while your partner listens with eyes closed. Try marching with heavy steps and then softly with light steps. Which sounds are easier to hear? Record your observations in your science journal.

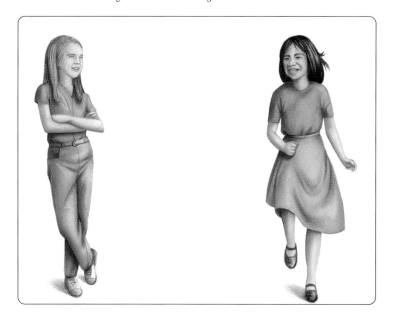

2. Wait for your partner to kneel down and press one ear lightly against the floor. March on the spot again. What does your partner hear?

3. Change places with your partner, and repeat steps 1 and 2. Record your observations.

Reflect on Your Results

1. In step 1, did the marching sound travel through the air? What proof do you have that it did?

2. In step 2, did the marching sound travel through the floor? What proof do you have that it did?

3. Did you notice anything else about the marching sound?

PART 3: SAY IT WITH STRING

1. Stand about 3 m away from your partner. Take turns speaking to each other. Try whispering and then speaking in a normal voice. Please don't shout.

2. Put one cup upside down on a table. Then, carefully punch a small hole in the bottom of it by pressing the nail into it. Repeat this with the other cup.

3. Put one end of the string through the hole from the outside of the cup. Tie a large knot at the end of the string so that it can't come out of the cup. Do this for both cups.

4. Stand about 3 m apart again with each of you holding one of the cups. Make sure the string is tight between the two cups. Speak into your cup while your partner holds the other cup to his or her ear. Try whispering and then speaking in a normal voice. Please don't shout.

Nails have sharp points. Be careful not to poke yourself or anyone else with one. Your teacher may make the holes in your cups with the nail for you so you don't accidentally hurt yourself.

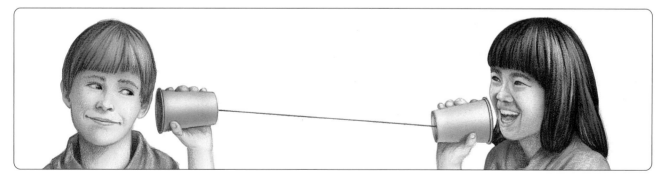

5. Take a turn being the one who listens, and repeat step 4. Record your observations in your science journal.

Reflect on Your Results

1. In step 1, did your voice travel through the air? What proof do you have that it did?

2. In steps 4 and 5, did the sound of your voice travel through the string? What proof do you have that it did?

3. Did you notice anything else about the voice sounds?

PART 4: SOUND IN WATER

1. Do this activity at home. Fill an aquarium or large glass bowl with water.

2. Tap the two small rocks together in the air.

3. Hold the two rocks under the water. Put your ear against the glass. Tap the rocks together under water. Record your observations in your science journal.

Reflect on Your Results

1. In step 2, did the tapping sound travel through the air? What proof do you have that it did?

2. In step 3, did the tapping sound travel through the water? What proof do you have that it did?

3. Did you notice anything else about the tapping sounds?

4. Discuss what you have discovered about the ability of sound to travel through air and other materials with your partner. Then, write a few sentences that describe your thoughts and observations about sound travel.

5. Compare your description with those of other classmates. How are your observations similar to theirs? different?

PART 5: IT'S YOUR TURN!

1. Design your own fair test (or series of tests) to answer this question: "Does sound travel better through some materials than others?" Test at least five different materials.

2. Record your results in a chart. Then, list the materials in order from the best material for sound to travel through to the worst. Write a sentence to summarize your answer. How could you check your answer?

Reflect on Your Results

1. What kinds of materials did you find sound travelled through best? What kinds of materials did you find sound travelled through worst? Discuss your findings with your classmates.

What Did You Learn?

1. How does sound get from its source to you?

2. How do you know that sound travels through air? through water? through solid materials such as wood and metal?

3. Put the following items in order from the best material for sound to travel through to the worst: milk, telephone pole, carbon dioxide gas. Explain the order of your list.

4. Why was it important for you to compare your observations and thoughts about sound travel with those of others in your class?

5. Read the Information Station. Then, think again about why having sound effects for spaceship engines in outer space is not scientifically correct. Why can't sound effects occur in space? Why do you think these sound effects are added to TV shows and movies anyway?

INFORMATION STATION

What Does Sound Need to Travel?

Sounds are vibrations caused by moving objects. For you to hear the sounds, the sound vibrations have to travel from their source to your ear. If your ear is under water, the vibrations have to travel through the water. If your ear is up against a brick wall, the vibrations have to travel through the solid brick. If your ear is in the air (like it is right now), the vibrations have to travel through the air.

Sound can do all this because sound needs a substance, or matter, to travel through. Bricks are solid matter. So are trees and bones and strings and wires. Water is liquid matter. So is soda pop and milk and motor oil and vinegar. Air is matter in the form of a gas. So is hydrogen and helium and carbon dioxide. Sound can travel through all these materials because they're all made of matter.

However, you've seen for yourself that sound can travel more easily through some kinds of matter than others.

Since sound needs matter to travel through, it can't travel in outer space. There's no matter in outer space between the planets, moons, stars, asteroids, and comets—not even invisible gases—for sound to travel through.

INVESTIGATING FURTHER

The Speed of Sound

How fast does sound travel? What speeds can it reach in gases? in liquids? in solids? Is there a limit to the speed of sound? Have people ever travelled at the speed of sound? Do some research to find the answers to these questions.

Now Hear This!

Sounds fill the air around us. Some soundscapes, like a busy downtown area, can be so full of sounds that it's almost painful to listen to. You might not even realize how much sound there is unless you go to a place that's quiet.

Imagine a soundscape that you enjoy. It could be a park, your bedroom, your classroom, or a barnyard—even a busy downtown area, if that's where you like to be. In your mind, hear all the sounds in the soundscape. Then, imagine pressing the mute button on a remote control that can turn off the sound vibrations.

What would it be like to see people moving their lips, or animals or cars moving around, and not hear anything? See if you can draw a picture to capture how it feels to be in a soundless place.

In **Getting Started** you will trace how one event can make other things happen. In **Let's Investigate** you will gather information about the parts of the ear and show how they work together to let you hear. In **Investigating Further** you can design a test to check how you "find" sounds with your ears.

GETTING STARTED

Think about the phrase "a chain of events". It's usually used to describe a series of events where something happens that in turn makes something else happen.

Look at this weird contraption, for example. Someone invented this machine for fun. It's supposed to do something simple, but in a very complicated way. Follow the chain of events. What's the source of all the action? What's the end result? How do sound vibrations fit into all this?

LET'S INVESTIGATE

You will need
● for Part 1: reference books and computer resources with information on the ear and hearing

Sound vibrations have to go through an amazing chain of events to reach your ear so that you can hear them. What are the links in this chain of events? How is your ear designed to let you hear?

First, collect information about the ear and how it detects vibrations. Then, create something to show the chain of events that allows you to hear.

PART 1: RESEARCHING THE HUMAN EAR

1. Use the following parts of the ear as keywords for your research:
   - anvil
   - auditory nerve ("auditory" comes from an ancient word that means "hearing")
   - auricle
   - cochlea
   - ear canal
   - ear drum
   - hammer
   - stirrup

2. Record your research.

You may want to create a chart to record the parts of the ear (structures) and what they do (functions). What other ways could you record the results of your research?

You may include information about any other parts of the ear you find in your research.

Parts of the Ear	
Structure	Function
anvil	

PART 2: DESIGNING A SOUND CHAIN

1. Look at all the information you collected about the structure and function of the parts of the ear. Think about how the parts of the ear are arranged and how they work together. Make and label a sketch showing the links between all the parts of the ear.

2. Use this information to show the chain of events that lets you hear. Choose one of the ways to show this listed below, or come up with your own way to do it.
   - If you like building things, you could construct a model of the ear. (If you're really adventurous, you could try making it a working model!)
   - If you like inventing stories, you could write about the adventures of the Vibration Family on their trip from a sound source through the human ear.

If you want to see one way to build a working model of the ear, look for
Sound
by Wendy Baker in **Make It Work! series** (Scholastic: Richmond Hill, ON, 1993).

- If you like drama or dancing, you could create a play or dance routine about the chain of sound events.
- If you like singing and music, you could compose a song about the sound chain.

What Did You Learn?

1. Write the following parts of the ear in the correct order (going from the outer ear to inside the ear): auditory nerve, cochlea, ear drum, auricle, stirrup, anvil, ear canal, hammer. How do you know your order is right?

2. In Now Hear This! you discovered that sounds can travel through solids, liquids, and gases. What role do these kinds of materials play in the sound chain?

3. Where was it easiest to find information? Which information was most complete? How might you do your research differently another time?

4. Read Science in Our Lives. Then, answer this question: "How is the way you hear similar to the way a recording is made on a compact disc, and how is it different?"

How Can the Cochlea Help You Understand Compact Discs?

The sound vibrations that reach the cochlea are changed into electricity-like signals that travel along the auditory nerve to the brain, which interprets these signals as sound. Recording sounds on a compact disc uses a similar process.

It starts with an instrument that you've probably heard of: a microphone. A small part inside the microphone vibrates when sound reaches it. This part changes the sound vibrations into electrical signals.

underside of disc

focused laser beam

laser

turntable drive motor

These signals are then sent to a laser in a kind of code that the laser can "read". The laser uses the coded signals to cut a circular track of extremely tiny pits onto the underside of a compact disc. There can be billions of these pits on each disc.

When you play a compact disc, a powerful beam of laser light shines on the underside of the disc. This light is reflected when it shines on the disc surface and is not reflected when it shines on a pit. A device inside the compact disc player changes the reflecting flashes into electrical signals, which are then turned into sound.

You can play a compact disc as many times as you like. A compact disc cannot be worn out since the pits on the underside don't rub against anything as it plays.

INVESTIGATING FURTHER

Specialized Ears

Start an animal ear collection. Find pictures of different animals to compare their ears. Look at the pictures, and see if you can figure out how their ears suit their way of life.

How do your ears help you locate sounds? Can you locate sounds better if they come from in front of you? from behind you? from beside you? Design a fair test to investigate these questions.

Do fish hear?

Loud and Soft

Imagine making a speech to hundreds of people in an auditorium using your normal speaking voice. It would be difficult to speak loud enough for everyone to hear you.

A microphone changes sound into electrical signals, which allow the energy of the sound vibrations to be boosted and the sound vibrations to become louder. Today, speakers can use microphones to make their voices heard.

You probably use a microphone nearly every day. Try to think where it might be.

In Getting Started you will explain one way to make sounds louder or softer. In Let's Investigate you will test many ways to make sounds louder and quieter. In Investigating Further you can learn how hearing aids work to help people hear.

GETTING STARTED

If you were the student in these pictures, what would the teacher's voice sound like? Discuss your ideas as a class. How can you find out how accurate your ideas are?

LET'S INVESTIGATE

In the experiments you did in Sound Travel, you discovered at least one way to make sounds louder. In what other ways can you make sounds louder?

PART 1: SNAP TO IT!

1. Snap your fingers, or clap your hands instead. Do it again, but do it louder. Do it again, but do it softer. Record what you did in your science journal.

1. How did you make the snapping or clapping sound louder and softer? (This may seem obvious, but that's okay. Science is often about explaining and understanding things that are obvious or simple.)

PART 2: IT'S A SNAP

1. Team up with a classmate. Stand beside your partner, and start snapping your fingers softly. Make sure your partner can hear the sound. Keep snapping, and start moving slowly until you are about 1 m away from your partner. What happens to the sound?

2. Keep snapping your fingers. Ask your partner to hold one end of the cardboard tube up to one ear with the tube pointed toward you. What happens to the sound? Record your observations in your science journal.

3. Change places with your partner, and repeat steps 1 and 2.

Reflect on Your Results

1. How can you bring a sound closer without moving either its source or your ear nearer to it? How do you think this works? Record your ideas in your science journal.

PART 3: FUNNELLING SOUND

1. Make a funnel by rolling a strong piece of paper into the shape of a cone. Use tape to hold the paper in this shape.

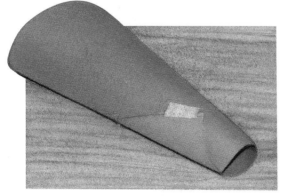

You will need
- for Part 2: at least one cardboard tube
- for Part 3: several square pieces of heavy paper of different sizes and tape
- for Part 4: your favourite funnels and a long tube (such as a garden hose, a length of plastic tubing, or a number of cardboard tubes taped together)

2. Hold the small end of the funnel up to your ear, and listen to the sounds in the room. What do you notice about the sounds in the room? Record your observations in your science journal.

3. Hold the small end of the funnel up to your mouth and whisper. You could also try this outside and speak in a normal voice. Ask your partner to start walking away from you. Mark the spot where your partner can no longer hear you. Measure or guess the distance from you to that spot in metres. Record your observations.

4. Make a different-sized funnel and repeat step 2.

5. Change places with your partner, and use the new funnel to repeat step 3.

6. Try making and experimenting with different-sized funnels.

Reflect on Your Results

1. How do different-sized funnels affect the sounds you make and hear through them?

2. What happens to the sound of your voice as it goes into the funnel? What happens to it when it reaches your partner's ear?

PART 4: TALKING THROUGH A TUBE

1. Attach a funnel to each end of the long tube. Stand fairly close to your partner, and whisper into your funnel while your partner listens through her or his funnel. Take turns whispering and listening.

2. Move apart from each other. Try having a whisper conversation again. When you can no longer hear each other, measure or guess the distance apart you are in metres. Record the distance in your science journal.

3. If your tube is bendable, see whether you can have a whisper conversation around corners. (If it isn't bendable, how could you construct a tube that is?)

1. How far could you send a whisper? How does this work? Record your ideas.

INFORMATION STATION

Sound on the Move...for a While

If you drop a pebble into a pond, you see ripples moving away from the spot you dropped it in all directions. These ripples don't keep moving away forever. As they get farther from where you dropped the pebble, they get smaller and smaller. Soon, you can't see them anymore.

Something similar happens with sound. When a sound source causes vibrations, the vibrations—or sound waves—move away from it in all directions. As they get farther from the source, they get weaker and weaker. For example, if you're standing next to a barking dog, the barking sounds are strong and noticeable. If you walk away from the dog and the dog keeps barking the same way, the barking sound will get weaker and weaker. It won't take long before you'll be so far away that you can't hear the barking at all. That's because the barking sound has gotten too weak to reach your ears.

When sounds are passed through a tube or funnel, the sounds don't spread out as much—so they stay stronger longer. This makes them seem louder.

A megaphone works in the same way as a tube or funnel. When you speak in a normal voice, the sound of your voice goes out in all directions. When you use a megaphone, the funnel of the megaphone sends most of the sound in one direction.

A microphone—like the one inside the mouthpiece of a telephone—also helps the sound of your voice stay stronger longer. What other devices help make sounds louder or last longer?

What Did You Learn?

1. What's one way to control the loudness or softness of a sound? (Hint: Reread your observations from part 1.)

2. Does using a tube or a funnel to listen to or send out sounds increase the loudness of those sounds? If so, how?

SCIENTISTS IN ACTION

Audiologists are scientists trained to help people of all ages who have a hearing loss. They use special devices called audiometers to measure hearing.

Alexander Graham Bell invented the first audiometer to help the hearing impaired. He also invented the photophone, a device that transmits speech using light rays. We still use a version of the photophone today. Do you know what it is?

Audiologists test and classify people's hearing to find out how much of a hearing loss they have and what is causing it. Audiologists then recommend ways to help people hear better, such as fitting a patient with a hearing aid. This small device fits in a person's ear and amplifies sound vibrations (makes the vibrations stronger).

SCIENCE IN OUR LIVES

Measuring Sound: Loudness and Softness

We measure the loudness and softness of sounds in units called decibels. These units are named after the scientist and inventor Alexander Graham Bell.

What decibel number do we give to the quietest sound that people can hear? What's the decibel number of normal speech? What's the decibel number of the loudest sound you have ever experienced? How would hearing that kind of loud sound a lot affect you?

Sound Source	Decibels
Space shuttle lift-off	175
Cannon firing (ear drum ruptures)	160
Jackhammer at one-metre distance (pain in ears)	140
Jet take-off, gunshot	130
Concert, loud thunder (discomfort)	120
Motorcycle at one-metre distance, car horn at one-metre distance, power saw	110
Loud piano playing, power mower, subway train, garbage disposal	100
Dog barking at one-metre distance, small truck accelerating, heavy traffic	90
Shouting at one-metre distance, loud radio, busy street traffic, ringing alarm clock	80
Vacuum cleaner, toilet flushing, dishwasher, air conditioner	70
Talking at one-metre distance, kitchen sounds	60
Quiet restaurant	50
City sounds at night, quiet home	40
Soft whisper, empty theatre	30
Rustling leaves	20
Quiet breathing	10
Quietest sound that people can hear	0

INVESTIGATING FURTHER

Hearing Aids

Collect information about hearing aids and how they help people hear. If possible, draw a diagram of a hearing aid or bring in a real hearing aid to examine.

High and Low

What is happening in this picture? What sound might the ruler be making? Imagine that the ruler is pushed farther over the edge of the desk and then flicked again. How might the sound be different? How can you find out?

Now imagine that the ruler is pulled back so that less of it sticks over the edge of the desk and then flicked again. How might the sound be different? Check your answer.

In **Getting Started** you will describe the difference between sounds. In **Let's Experiment** you will use different materials to find ways to make different sounds. In **Investigating Further** you can learn about special sounds called ultrasound.

GETTING STARTED

Listen as

- a classmate says something in a deep voice and then a high voice
- your teacher plays two different sounds on a tube-type musical instrument
- your teacher plays two different sounds on a stringed musical instrument

How are the two sounds different in each case? What do you think causes this difference?

LET'S EXPERIMENT

Have you ever thought about how you control sounds to make them higher and lower? Here's your chance to play with high and low sounds.

First, read through all of the experiments. Predict the results of the experiment at each station. Then, visit each station and test your predictions.

STATION A: POP MUSIC

These students are taking turns blowing across the top of an empty bottle and listening to the sound that makes. In a moment, they will pour some water into the same bottle and blow across the top again. Predict what kind of sound they will hear. Will it be the same? higher? lower? Write your answers in your science journal.

1. Let one person in your group blow across the top of the empty bottle. Listen to the sound the blowing makes.

2. Take turns blowing across the top of the bottle.

3. Pour some water into the bottle (until it is about one-quarter full). Take turns blowing across the top of the bottle and listening to the sound the blowing makes. Record your observations in your science journal.

4. Repeat step 3, but fill the bottle with water until it is about half full.

TIP

Reread the introduction on page 100. Think about how a ruler vibrates when different lengths of it are flicked. Think about the sounds these different lengths make when they vibrate.

You will need
- for station A: a pitcher of water, a glass bottle, and paper towels
- for station B: 6 nails hammered into a block of wood
- for station C: 6 different-sized drums made from cardboard tubes, balloon pieces, and elastic bands
- for station D: elastic bands (different sizes and thicknesses) and books of different sizes
- for station E: a pitcher of water, a glass bottle, and paper towels

STATION B: NAIL XYLOPHONE

These students are taking turns tapping each nail with a pencil and listening to the sound it makes. How will the sounds each nail makes be different? Record your predictions in your science journal.

1. Take turns tapping each nail with a pencil. Record your observations in your science journal.

STATION C: BALLOON CONGAS

These students are taking turns tapping each drum with a pencil and listening to the sound it makes. How will the sound each drum makes be different? Record your predictions in your science journal.

1. Take turns tapping each drum with a pencil. Record your observations in your science journal.

STATION D: ELASTIC STRING BAND

These students are taking turns plucking different sizes of stretched elastics and listening to the sounds they make. How will the sounds made from the thick elastic bands compare with those made from the thin ones? How will the sounds made from very tightly stretched elastic bands compare with the sounds of less tightly stretched ones? Record your predictions in your science journal.

1. Choose an elastic. Put it around the longest part of a large book. Then, pluck it with your finger.

2. Use the same elastic, and repeat step 1 with books of different sizes. Record your observations.

3. Listen to the plucking sounds that other people in your group make with thinner and thicker elastics when they do steps 1 and 2. Record your observations.

STATION E: GLASS CHIMES

This looks a bit like station A, but there's a difference. These students are taking turns tapping the bottle near the bottom with a pencil. In a moment, they will pour some water into the bottle and tap it again. What kind of sound will they hear? Will it be the same? higher? lower? What would happen to the sound if they poured more water into the bottle? Record your predictions in your science journal.

1. Tap the empty glass bottle with a pencil.

2. Let another group member add water to the bottle and tap it again.

3. Take turns adding water to and tapping the bottle. Record your observations in your science journal.

Reflect on Your Results

1. Copy and complete each of the following statements in your science journal. Give proof to show that you have completed each statement correctly.

   ● When a vibrating object is shorter, the sound it creates is...
   ● When a vibrating object is thinner, the sound it creates is...
   ● When a vibrating object is tighter, the sound it creates is...
   ● When a vibrating object is taller, the sound it creates is...
   ● When a vibrating object is thicker, the sound it creates is...
   ● When a vibrating object is looser, the sound it creates is...

What Did You Learn?

1. Read the Information Station. Give two examples of how you can increase the pitch of a sound.

2. Give two examples of how you can decrease the pitch of a sound.

3. Look at this drawing. Imagine that you tapped each nail with the same amount of strength. Which nail would make the highest-pitched sound? Which nail would make the lowest-pitched sound?

4. Why do scientists test the same thing several times?

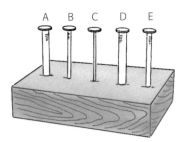

INFORMATION STATION

High and Low, Loud and Soft

Different kinds of vibrations result in different kinds of sounds: loud sounds, soft sounds, high sounds, and low sounds. Here's how scientists explain it.

Vibrations are back-and-forth movements. Scientists talk about the frequency of vibrations. Frequency means how often the back-and-forth movements happen in a certain amount of time. A high frequency means that there are more vibrations every second, which is a high sound. A lower frequency means that there are fewer vibrations every second, which is a low sound. Remember when you thought about flicking a ruler at the beginning of this learning event. The ruler was vibrating.

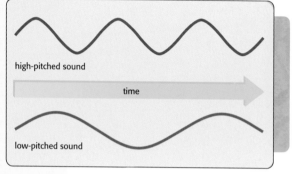

Scientists use the word **pitch** to talk about high and low sounds. A scientist would say that higher-pitched sounds have higher frequencies. What sounds have lower frequencies?

The top diagram may help you picture the difference between high-pitched and low-pitched sounds.

How do scientists talk about loud and soft sounds? Think about the activities you did in Loud and Soft. You got louder sounds when you made them stronger. (What did you do to make them stronger?) You got softer sounds when you made them weaker. (How did you do that?)

In the bottom diagram, notice that the louder sound has the same frequency as the softer sound. However, something is different about their sound waves. Look at the louder sound. The waves are taller, aren't they? Now look at the softer sound. The waves are smaller. That's how the vibrations of loud and soft sounds are different.

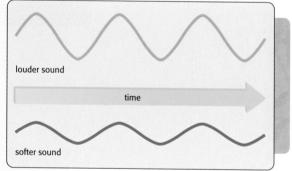

SCIENTISTS IN ACTION

Elephants have been a part of human history in many cultures for thousands of years. They have been kept in zoos, kept as pets, honoured as sacred beings, filmed, and studied. However, in the 1980s science discovered something new about elephants.

A scientist named Katharine Payne was observing some elephants at a zoo. She noticed that she could feel vibrations, even though she wasn't hearing any sounds. Could the vibrations be coming from the elephants? Maybe, she thought, elephants can communicate with each other using sounds so low-pitched that we humans can't hear them.

Payne and other scientists did research that provides proof to support this idea. They found that elephants, like whales, use low-pitched sounds that vibrate too slowly for us—and most other animals—to hear. The low-frequency vibrations of this infrasound, as it's called, travel really well. Elephants can send infrasound messages over distances of four kilometres. Scientists suspect that the infrasound messages can travel even farther—maybe even twice as far!

INVESTIGATING FURTHER

Ultrasound

In Scientists in Action you learned that we call the low-frequency sound below the range of human hearing infrasound. We call the high-frequency sound above our range of hearing ultrasound. Find out more about ultrasound and about the technologies that let us use it, even though we can't hear it.

On Guard Against Noise

Some sounds are pleasant to hear, and others aren't. Which of these sounds would you enjoy listening to? Which ones would make you want to cover your ears? Some sounds start off as pleasant ones and then become unpleasant ones. How? What about the other way around?

In Getting Started you will begin to explain the difference between pleasant sounds and noise. In Let's Investigate you will develop a solution to a noise problem around your school. In Investigating Further you can design a soundproof study room.

GETTING STARTED

Where might you have you seen this kind of sign? Why do some places have signs about keeping noise levels down? What is noise, anyway? How do you think noise affects people?

Create a list or "rule book" to describe your ideas about what makes a pleasant sound and what makes a noise. Compare your list with a classmate's list. Which choices do you agree or disagree on?

LET'S INVESTIGATE

Have you ever felt like a place you had to be in was too noisy? Did you wish you could change that? Plan a campaign to control noise levels in or around your school.

1. Brainstorm as a class about the noise problems in and around your school. Choose a student volunteer to record each problem on the chalkboard.

2. Decide which noise problem is the worst and which one is the easiest to live with. Make a list of the noise problems in order from worst to easiest to live with.

3. In a small group, choose one of the worst noise problems you believe you can solve. Decide how you would like to gather information to help you solve it. You may choose to talk to people in and around the school who are affected by this problem. If so, ask them for suggestions about how to solve it, and record their suggestions in your science journal. You may decide to design a survey sheet with questions and ask these people to fill it out for you.

4. Gather information on the noise problem you want to solve.

5. Look at the information your group has gathered. Does it give you new ideas about what the problem is?

6. Make a plan to tackle the noise problem, and put your plan into action.

7. Keep a diary of the work you do every day. Set a time each day for your group to share their diary entries so that you know what everyone is doing. Discuss any problems that group members may have with the work.

8. When your noise-reduction campaign is finished, do a follow-up survey with the people you talked to or surveyed. Ask them how they feel about the noise problem now. How do you feel about it now?

Reflect on Your Results

1. Use your group's diaries to create a timeline that shows what your group did and what happened during your campaign.

2. Share your timeline with other groups. How did they solve their noise problem? Which of their ideas or strategies do you really like? Why?

Use the Internet to find out about organizations concerned about noise control. Share your discoveries with your class.

What Did You Learn?

1. Are high-pitched sounds always noise? What about low-pitched sounds? loud sounds? soft sounds? How do pitch and loudness relate to "noise"?

2. What makes some sounds noise?

3. If you had to plan a new strategy for your group's noise problem, would you do anything differently? Why?

INVESTIGATING FURTHER

Blocking Sound

Design a soundproof study room for use by students who want to read and do homework in peace and quiet at school. The room should be big enough to hold 10 desks comfortably. Assume that the room set aside for this has

- hard concrete walls and a hard wooden floor
- a large window that lets in traffic noise from a busy nearby street
- a door through which you can hear the footsteps of people walking along the hall outside—even when the door is shut

Recall what you already know about sound. Decide what else you need to learn to help you solve the problem. Then, draw up plans for soundproofing this room. See if you can find real samples of the materials you want to use and include them with your design. Otherwise, cut out or draw pictures of these materials.

How are opera houses or music halls designed to keep street noise from being heard inside? How are they designed to keep their music from being heard in the street? Use reference materials to find out how noise can be absorbed. How could these design features help reduce noise at school or at home?

Sound Symphony

What roles does sound play in your life? What devices do you use that make sound? How can you control the sounds they make? Which sounds serve a useful purpose?

In Getting Started you will examine some musical instruments to see how they work. In Let's Investigate you will invent your own sound maker. In Investigating Further you can research the areas of sound you find most interesting.

GETTING STARTED

Some students decided to form their own band using home-made musical instruments. Here are a few of the instruments they invented. How do you think these instruments work? How can the students control the loudness and pitch of the sounds these instruments make? How might you make these instruments work better?

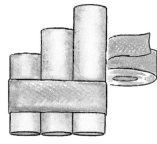

LET'S INVESTIGATE

You will need
- parts for a sound maker

Some sound makers, like a tuning fork, are designed to make only one pitch of sound. Many kinds of drums are designed that way, too. Can you think of ways to change the pitch of these, and other, sound makers?

In this activity, you get to invent your own sound maker.

1. Decide what kind of sound maker you want to invent. For example, you might want to invent
   - a stringed instrument like a guitar or violin
   - a blowing instrument like a recorder or a trumpet
   - a tapping instrument like a drum or a xylophone
   - a device that sounds like cars and trucks driving down the street

2. Collect the parts you will need to make your instrument or device. Make sure you will be able to control the pitch and the loudness of your sound maker's sounds.

3. Plan how you will put your sound maker's parts together.

4. When you're finished, write a small instruction booklet to tell other people how to use your sound maker. Include pictures to help them understand your instructions. Try using some of your classmates' sound makers, and let them try to use yours. Can you follow each other's instructions about how to use the sound makers?

Reflect on Your Results

1. How did you design your sound maker so that you could change the pitch of its sounds?

2. How did you design your sound maker so that you could change the loudness of its sounds?

3. Could your classmates use your sound maker in the way you intended?

SCIENTISTS IN ACTION

You may have heard of the American inventor and politician Benjamin Franklin. He's the person who discovered that lightning is electricity. Perhaps you didn't know that he invented a musical instrument. It's called the glass harmonica.

The glass harmonica consists of a variety of bowl-like glasses that sit on a turning device. The rims of the glasses are kept wet as they turn. A musician plays the glasses by holding a finger against the wet rim, which creates a haunting sound. Try it for yourself! You will need to use good-quality drinking glasses. Wipe both the glass rim and your finger with vinegar first to remove any oil and dirt on them. Then, wet the rim and your finger with water. Slowly rub your finger around the rim. Be patient. You'll know when you've created the right sound.

▼ Glass Orchestra

Glass harmonicas were very popular 200 to 300 years ago. In fact, the great composer Wolfgang Amadeus Mozart wrote music for this instrument.

Today, very few people play the glass harmonica in public performances. One of the few exceptions is a Canadian quartet of musicians called the Glass Orchestra. If you think that they play the music that they compose on glass, you're right!

What Did You Learn?

1. Use what you learned by inventing sound makers and by reading about the Glass Orchestra to try making and playing some glass music. You'll be amazed by the sounds you can create!

INVESTIGATING FURTHER

What Else Would You Like to Learn?

You've barely scratched the surface in your study of sound. Do you want to know about echoes? What about modern communication technologies and how they code, send, and decode sound messages? Did you know that one of the most popular electronic musical instruments, the synthesizer, has a Canadian connection? Pick something that "sounds" interesting to you, and find out more about it. There are uncharted soundscapes waiting for you!

Thinking About Soundscapes

1. Explain how sound travels to your ears and how you hear it. You can use words and pictures. Include as many parts of the ear as you can.

2. Name three types of matter that sound travels easily through. Give examples of them.

3. Why does a megaphone make the sound of a person's voice louder?

4. Draw a poster showing harmful levels of sound around us.

Inventor's Workshop

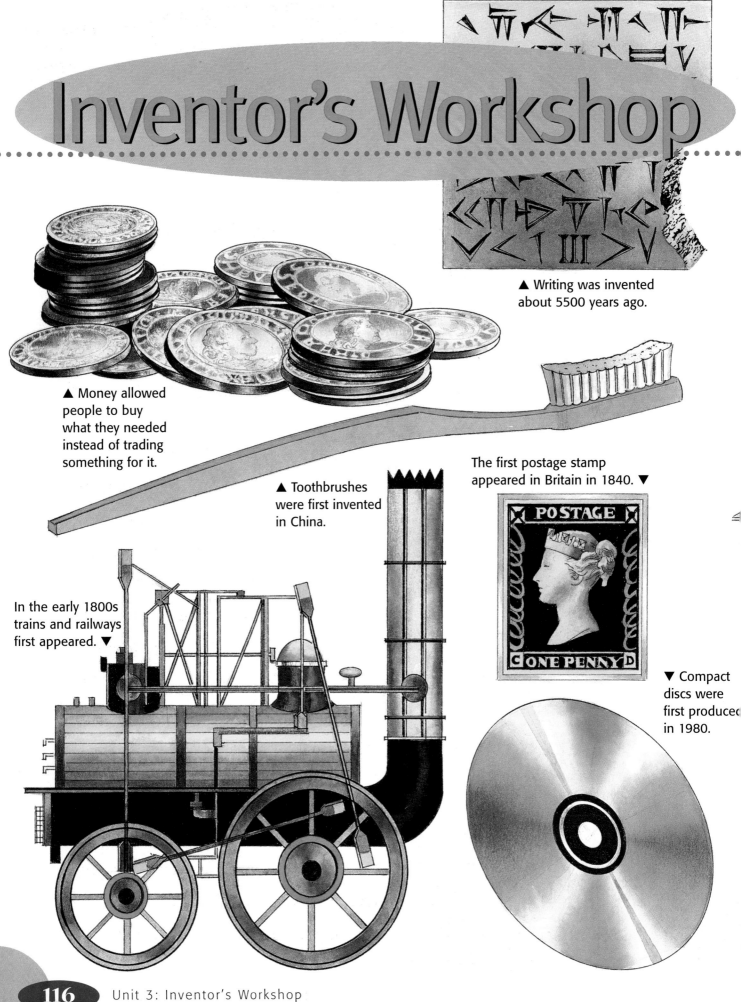

▲ Writing was invented about 5500 years ago.

▲ Money allowed people to buy what they needed instead of trading something for it.

▲ Toothbrushes were first invented in China.

The first postage stamp appeared in Britain in 1840. ▼

POSTAGE
ONE PENNY

In the early 1800s trains and railways first appeared. ▼

▼ Compact discs were first produced in 1980.

▲ Oil lamps have been used for about 20 000 years.

◄ Stone tools were made by chipping a rock called flint until its edge was very sharp.

▼ In 1981 the first space shuttle flew.

From the beginning of time, people have been inventing. At first people invented things to help them survive. Clothes and tools, such as axes and knives, were some of the earliest inventions. Now people invent all kinds of things for all kinds of reasons.

Look around your classroom. What inventions can you see? Inventions are not only things but also the materials an object is made of, the design of an object, or the use of the object.

Coming up with a clever idea is part of inventing, but inventors do more than come up with clever ideas. They design, experiment, make changes, and perfect their ideas. It usually takes persistence and lots of time to create an invention.

In this unit you will discover the stages of inventing. At each stage you will apply what you have learned to develop an invention of your own.

What Is the Problem?

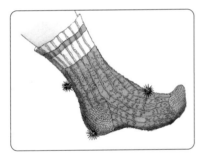

Read about these inventions and decide what problem you will solve with an invention.

Inventions exist because someone had an idea that he or she thought could work. But where did the idea come from?

Sometimes we have a problem or a need and we invent something to solve the problem. For example, in 1810 Bryan Donkin invented the tin can to meet a particular need: to preserve food on long trips. The earliest cans were opened with a chisel—a messy job! About 50 years after tin cans were invented, that problem was solved as well. The first can opener was patented.

Sometimes an invention happens by accident. Floating soap was invented in 1878 by a worker at Procter & Gamble who forgot to turn off a machine that stirred soap. Air bubbles mixed with the soap and made it so light that it floated. Customers liked the new soap.

Some inventions are adapted from something that already exists or are copied from nature. Hook-and-loop fasteners such as Velcro were invented by copying from nature. A Swiss engineer studied the burrs that stuck to his socks after walking in the woods, and he copied the idea to make fabric fasteners.

Some inventions are actually new uses for things that already exist. The original Frisbee was a metal pie plate used by the Frisbie Pie Company in Bridgeport, Connecticut. Students at nearby Yale University invented Frisbee throwing when they tossed the plates back and forth after eating the pies. Walter Morrison produced the first plastic models in the 1950s, and Frisbee games and competitions became widespread.

LEARNING ABOUT INVENTING

WHERE DO INVENTIONS COME FROM?

You will need
● books and other resources about inventions

1. Look at each of these inventions. What problem does it solve? Why is it made of that material? How does its shape or design make it suitable for its purpose?

2. Choose an invention—an object in your classroom or home—and research its history. Write the headings How, Who, Why, and When in four sections of a page. Now answer the following questions on the page: How was the object invented? Who invented it? Why? When? You can find information about inventions in books, in magazines, and on the Internet.

3. Share your research with two or three classmates. Ask them to write down any questions they have about the invention you researched. Do more research to find the answers to their questions.

4. Discuss with your classmates what you learned about how inventions are created. What did you learn about why things are invented?

FOR YOUR PROJECT

What Is the Problem?

You will work with a small group of classmates throughout this unit to invent something. To begin, survey your family and friends about problems they would like to have solved or inventions they would find useful.

1. With your group, brainstorm a list of questions you could ask to find out what problems people encounter in their everyday lives. For example, would they like to save time when they do a certain task? Do you want ideas about a specific kind of invention, for example, ones for a kitchen or a classroom, ones that are safe for the environment, or ones that could be used in space?

While you work on your invention, keep notes of all your ideas, discussions, and experiments in your science journal. It is important to keep a careful record of how your invention was developed. If something goes wrong, you can review your notes to find out where the problem occurred. Keep the notes you made about inventing. You can use them to help you develop other inventions later.

2. Decide on the best three to five questions, and write your survey. Everyone in your group will use the same questions for their survey.

3. Survey at least five people. Add your own answers to the survey questions.

4. Discuss the results of your survey in your group. Which problems do people want solved?

5. Which problems could be solved with an invention?

6. Which problem would you most like to solve?

7. Choose an idea that you would like to develop as your project for this unit. Record your idea in your science journal.

Reflect on Your Results

1. Describe some of the ways that inventors find ideas for new inventions.

2. What do you think is the hardest part about finding an idea for an invention?

3. How do inventions change over time?

4. What invention is very important to your life? Why?

INVENTORS HALL OF FAME

In 1897, George Washington Carver began a job helping cotton farmers in the United States learn more about farming. He soon discovered that growing peanuts on a farm one year made the soil better for growing cotton the next year. Soon many farmers in the southern United States were growing peanuts to improve their soil. In fact, they grew more peanuts than they could sell. Carver then invented 325 uses for peanuts—everything from peanut butter to printer's ink—so that farmers could sell all of their peanuts. What was the problem that he helped to solve with these inventions?

Choose a Solution

In the previous learning event, you decided on a problem that you would like to solve. Now you can think of a way to solve the problem.

Keep your eyes open. You never know where you will find a solution to your problem.

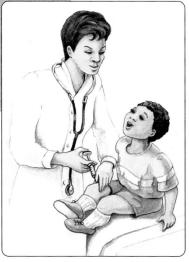

▲ In Canada, almost all children are vaccinated to prevent them from getting many serious diseases.

INVENTORS HALL OF FAME

In the 1790s, many people in Britain were dying of a disease called smallpox. Edward Jenner was a country doctor who tried to help many of these sick people. He remembered an old folk tale that said that anyone who got the mild disease cowpox would not get the much more serious disease smallpox. Jenner noticed that the old saying seemed to be true for his patients. He tested it by giving cowpox to a small boy. When the boy had recovered, he tried to give him smallpox, but the boy did not get sick! Jenner began giving people small amounts of cowpox to prevent them from getting smallpox. He had invented vaccinations!

Once an inventor decides to solve a problem with an invention, what happens? Often, an inventor will think of all the possible ways the invention could work. Then the inventor could think about the problems the invention would solve (pros) and the problems the invention might cause (cons).

Many inventors list the pros and cons of their invention so that they can evaluate the invention carefully.

Hugh Moore invented the paper cup in 1908 in New England to hold an individual serving of water. The paper cup gained popularity when new laws banned "sippers"—tin cups that people drank water from in public places that were seldom washed and were believed to spread disease. Individual paper cups provided a healthy alternative.

Sometimes two or more solutions to a problem may seem equally good. Then what would you do?

You could analyze the points on your list of pros and cons and decide which ones are more important and which ones are less important. For example, an idea may be inexpensive to make, but it may be dangerous. Inventors must consider all these factors when they choose the best idea to develop.

LEARNING ABOUT INVENTING

NEW SOLUTIONS AND NEW PROBLEMS

You will need
- a paper cup
- scissors
- glue
- adhesive tape

In your group, examine and discuss the paper cup.

1. What is a paper cup usually used for? What problems does it solve? What problems does it cause?

2. What else could you make or do with a paper cup? List at least four ideas. Write down what problem is solved by each idea. In your science journal, write down what problem is caused by each idea.

What Can We Do With a Paper Cup?			
Idea	Problem Solved	Pros	Cons

3. Evaluate the ideas by comparing the list of pros and cons for each idea.

4. Which idea does your group think is the best? Why?

Which factors were the most important to you when you were deciding which idea was the best? Why?

INVENTIONS IN OUR LIVES

Some inventions cause more problems than they solve. The self-cleaning house, invented by Frances Gabe, sounds like a good idea. Gabe developed an apparatus that fits in a box in the ceiling of each room and cleans the room with soapy water, rinses the room, and dries it. It also heats and cools the room. The invention also includes water-tight containers and covers for furniture, and self-cleaning kitchen cupboards. The self-cleaning house, however, is still not very popular. Would you buy one? Why or why not?

FOR YOUR PROJECT

Choose a Solution

Develop the idea for your group's invention.

1. In your group, brainstorm inventions to solve the problem you chose.

2. Choose the best three ideas, and list the problems that each idea solves and the problems that each idea causes.

3. Use the list of pros and cons to evaluate each idea.

4. As a group, decide on the best invention to develop.

Reflect on Your Results

1. What problems did you come across when you were developing an idea for your invention? How did you solve them?

2. How does working in a group make inventing easier? more difficult?

124

Design It to Work

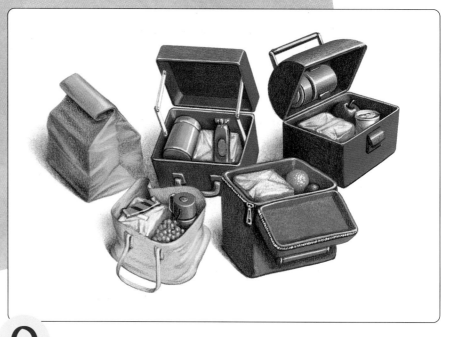

Once an inventor has an idea and has evaluated the pros and cons, it's time to design the invention. In this learning event, you will design an invention that will solve a problem.

An inventor thinks about an invention in different ways and considers many questions in producing the design: How will people use the invention? How easy should it be to use? How strong should it be? How much will it cost to make? How will it affect the environment? Finding answers to these questions helps an inventor decide how to design the invention.

Many designs can often serve the same purpose. For example, there are many ways to carry your lunch to school.

Once an inventor has chosen a design, the next step is often to make a prototype of the invention. A prototype is the first or an early model of something. Building the prototype will help the inventor assess the design and note the changes needed to improve the invention.

INVENTORS HALL OF FAME

Margaret Knight is most well known for inventing a machine in the 1860s to make flat-bottomed paper bags. Her prototype for the machine was made of wood. Although she made hundreds of bags with the machine, she knew the machine would have to be made of iron in order to get a patent. Yet the process of developing the design for an iron machine was complicated. By the time she did design one, her machine had been copied by Charles Annan who received a patent for it. After years of appealing to the Patent Office with the help of a lawyer, Knight proved that the design was hers, and she was granted the patent.

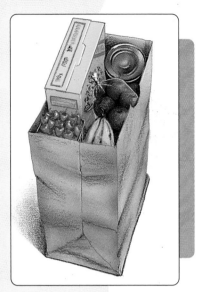

That was only one of many inventions that Knight had patented over her lifetime, mostly in the field of automotive engineering. She came up with her first useful invention at the age of 12. When she saw a weaver injured by a shuttle that flew off his loom, she invented a device to prevent such an injury. As the most famous woman inventor of her time, Knight was known as "Lady Edison", after inventor Thomas Edison.

LEARNING ABOUT INVENTING

DESIGNING FOR A PURPOSE

Your group will design something to keep an egg from breaking when it is dropped from a height of one metre.

1. With your group, design an invention to protect an egg when it is dropped. Sketch your invention in your science journal. Your design should use materials that you will be able to find easily.

2. Collect the materials that you will need.

List five things that make instructions easy to follow.

3. Build your invention.

4. Place an egg in it, and test it by dropping the invention from a height of one metre. How well did it work?

5. Write instructions and draw diagrams for building your design.

6. Exchange instructions with another group, and try to follow their instructions to build their design.

7. Explain to the other group which parts of their instructions were most helpful and which parts might need to be clearer.

FOR YOUR PROJECT

Design It to Work

With your group, make a sketch of your invention.

1. Discuss with others in your small group how you see your invention.

2. On your own, make a rough sketch of the invention. Include any details and information that you think will help others understand how the object will look and work.

3. Share your sketch with others in your group. Discuss each student's design. Which features are common to all of the designs? Which features do you think will work the best?

4. Combine the best ideas in a final sketch of the invention. Decide who will draw the final sketch.

5. Copy and complete this chart to describe the details of your invention.

Design Details				
Shape	Size	Uses	Materials	Overall Looks

Reflect on Your Results

1. What was the most difficult part of making a sketch of your idea? What was the easiest?

2. How much detail should a design of an invention include?

3. What new ideas about your invention developed as you sketched it?

INVENTORS HALL OF FAME

An observant tourist in New York City noticed that a streetcar driver was getting cold because he had to reach outside the streetcar to clear the snow off the windshield. The image of that cold driver stuck in Mary Anderson's mind when she returned to Alabama, and she began to work on her solution for the problem. She designed a long scraping arm to be attached to the outside of the window. It would have a handle on the inside for the driver to turn back and forth to clean the window. This device would allow the driver to stay warm. Anderson's invention was patented in 1903, but was rejected by the only company that she sent it to, and the device was never manufactured. This was Anderson's only invention.

After the patent lapsed, a mechanical windshield wiper—a different design for the same solution—was invented and registered in 1916.

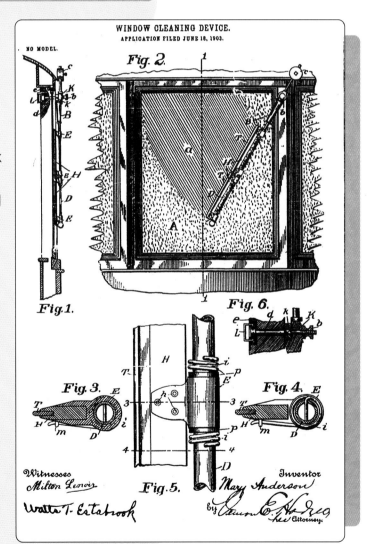

Tests and More Tests

Finally the inventor has a picture of the invention. But there's still a lot of work to do. Most inventors will test the materials to make sure they have chosen the right ones. As you test the materials for your invention, think carefully about what you need them to do.

Materials are an important part of any invention. The materials must do their job properly for the invention to be a success. Thomas Edison worked for years and tested thousands of materials to use as the filament in light bulbs before he finally found the right one.

Edison's light bulb ▼

▲ a modern light bulb

LEARNING ABOUT INVENTING

TESTING, TESTING, TESTING

You will choose the best tape to use to hang something from a wall.

Imagine that you have just invented this device to hang things on a wall. What kind of tape will be best for your design?

1. In your group, design an experiment to test which type of tape is the best for hanging something from a paper clip on a wall. Remember: in a fair test, everything about the experiment must stay the same; only the type of tape will change. How many paper clips will you need in order to test the tape? Where will you position each paper clip? What will you hang from each paper clip? What types of tape will you try?

2. Carry out the experiment. Record your observations.

3. What do the results of the experiment tell you? How well did you answer your question?

4. List the pros and cons of each type of tape. List two or three things you might use each type of tape for.

You will need
- paper clips
- different kinds of tape such as adhesive tape, masking tape, duct tape, and electrical tape

Write down your procedure (the steps you followed) to test the materials. Did you do exactly the same test for every kind of tape? What would you do differently if you did the experiment again?

Write down the steps in the experiment you designed. Record your observations and results for each material.

FOR YOUR PROJECT

Tests and More Tests

Design a test to find the best materials to use to build your invention.

1. List the materials you could use in your invention. Beside each item on your list, write why you have chosen that material (because it is flexible, strong, waterproof, and so on).

2. Choose what you want to test for to decide which materials would work best. Choose at least three materials to test.

3. How will you test the materials? Design a fair experiment.

4. Carry out the experiment. Record your observations and results in your science journal.

5. What materials will you use? Why?

Reflect on Your Results

1. Why is it important to test materials before building an invention?

2. Your tests helped you learn which materials worked best. What else might you want to know about the materials before you decide which ones to use?

Sir Sandford Fleming is one of Canada's most distinguished inventors and scientists, known best for creating the international system of time zones, designing Canada's first stamp, and engineering Canada's first railways.

He is not as well-known for inventing one of the first in-line skates. Although other models can be traced to the eighteenth century, Fleming was not aware of any others when he designed, built, and tested his prototype in 1845 at the age of 18. He built the prototype with wooden wheels. After testing, Fleming recommended using cast-iron wheels. What difference do you think the materials made?

This skate was tried with two wheels screwed in a piece wood. it did fine considering the wheels two narrow & too little dia. It is believed a skate something like the drawing would do very well (cast iron whe

Build It!

You've reached the stage where all of your ideas, planning, and experimentation come together into building your invention. It's time to construct a model of your invention.

LEARNING ABOUT INVENTING

LOOKING AT OTHER INVENTIONS

1. Discuss these inventions:

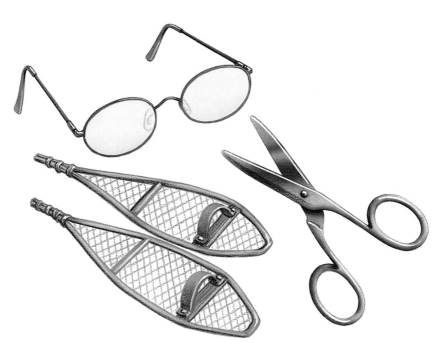

2. Record your observations about each invention. What is it used for? What problem did the invention solve? How does the design make the invention work? How might the design be improved? What materials are used? What other materials could have been used?

INVENTIONS IN OUR LIVES

The bicycle is an invention that has been refined over thousands of years and has been improved by many other inventions. The original idea goes back as far as 1200 B.C., when an Egyptian invented a two-wheeled vehicle powered by the rider's feet pushing the ground. A two-wheeler without pedals was reinvented in Germany in 1817. The first pedals—ones that moved back and forth rather than in circles—were added in 1839 by a Scottish blacksmith. A vet in Belfast invented air-filled tires in 1888. Other inventors changed steering methods, wheel sizes, brakes, solar power, gears, and a wide variety of materials. Years after the first bicycle was built, the design is still being changed.

FOR YOUR PROJECT

Build It!

1. Gather the materials and tools that you will need to build a model or prototype of your invention.

2. Decide how your model should be put together. Write out the steps involved.

3. Decide who will do each step. You may wish to have an adult help you.

4. Build your invention.

Record each step you followed to build your model. Write the instructions so that someone else could build your model by following the steps. Evaluate your invention. How well does it work?

Reflect on Your Results

1. What was the most difficult part of building your invention? What might have made it easier?

2. What was the most difficult part of the building process to describe in instructions? Try using a diagram to explain that part.

Tell the World

Plan how to market your invention.

An invention that isn't used isn't much good. To encourage people to use an invention, people need to hear about it. This is called marketing an invention.

Marketing should tell people how the invention would be useful to them.

INVENTORS HALL OF FAME

Acetylsalicylic acid, now commonly known as aspirin, was invented in France in 1853 by Charles Frederick Gerhardt. His invention was a laboratory version of salicin that came from the bark of a willow tree and was popular for treating fever. Gerhardt did not believe that his invention was an improvement over the natural salicin, so he did not market it. The invention was ignored for the next 40 years. In 1899, the Bayer company began marketing it and later marketed more convenient aspirin tablets. Now aspirin is known around the world.

LEARNING ABOUT INVENTING

WHY DO WE BUY?

With your group, discuss products that you like. What do you like about them? How are they packaged? How are they advertised? How are slogans used? What difference does a name make?

FOR YOUR PROJECT

Tell the World

If you want people to use your invention, you need to tell them why it is useful.

Describe the features of your invention in your science journal. What features did you highlight in your marketing idea? Describe your marketing idea in your science journal. Use as much detail as you can.

1. How does your invention solve the problem that it was invented to solve?

2. Who do you think would use your invention? What do they want to hear about it? How does it improve their lives? What is it about the appearance that is appealing to users?

3. Design a way to market your invention. It could be a poster, a product label, a radio or television commercial, a billboard, or a brochure. What is the name of your product? Will you ask a famous person to talk about it? Will you have a slogan? Remember to whom you are trying to sell it.

4. Present your marketing idea to your classmates.

Reflect on Your Results

1. Why did you choose the marketing idea you did? Explain why it will be a good way to let people know about your invention.

2. What new ideas did you get by watching others present their marketing ideas?

INVENTIONS IN OUR LIVES

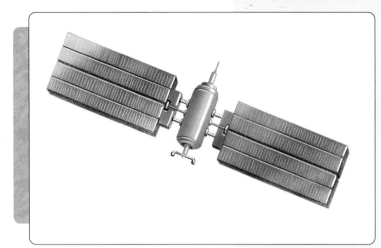

Today people are inventing more things than ever. Inventors are developing machines to make energy from the sun and the wind into energy we can use to heat and light our homes. A successful design will provide a lot of energy and be able to store some of it for cloudy or windless days.

Along the same lines, today's inventors are working hard to design cars and other vehicles that use less fuel.

Where else are inventions needed in today's world? Will you be one of the people to design one?

INVENTORS HALL OF FAME

David Zakutin recently invented a baseball with a computer inside it. The computer can tell you how quickly you threw the ball! Read what Zakutin has to say about inventing.

Question: How long did it take to get the first speed-sensing baseball to work?

Answer: About eight months.

Question: How many designs did you go through before you got to the final one?

Answer: Three. First I tried an all-plastic ball with a cover sewn around it. Then I tried to shrink the components to make it cost less to produce. Finally, I bought a baseball off the shelf and just put a hole in it.

Question: Inventing something is just the beginning, isn't it? What is happening now that you have invented something that works?

Answer: It's just a matter of showing it to the world, really. That is not easy, though. It's just like introducing yourself to the whole world.

Question: So, to be an inventor, you have to be patient?

Answer: Patient, for sure. And I think what makes a successful inventor is being willing to start over again from scratch. Not do it once, but maybe 10 times...and not complain.

Thinking About Inventor's Workshop

1. What two problems would you like an invention to help you solve?

2. What problems would this invention solve? What problems might it cause?

3. What two inventions could you not live without? Why?

4. What qualities make someone a good inventor?

5. What invention do you think has changed the world the most? Why?

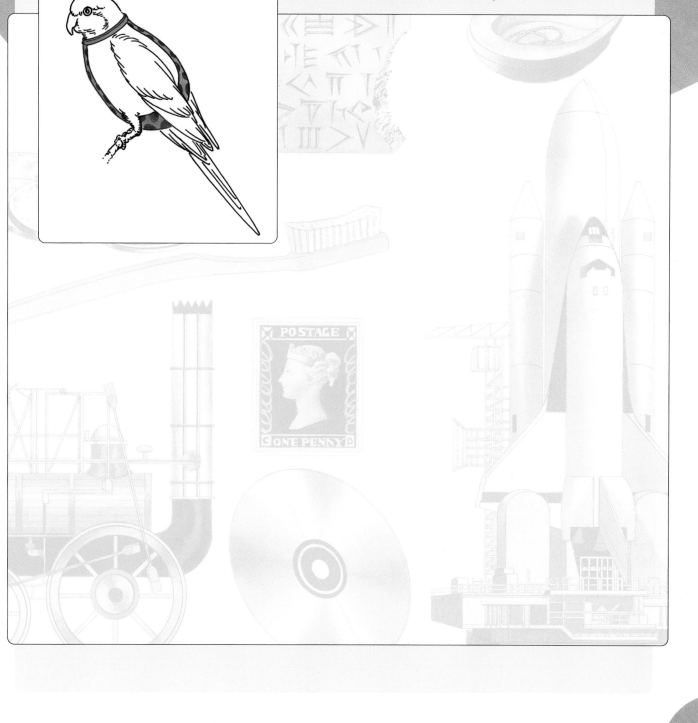

Light Show

Just about everywhere you look, light is putting on a show for you. There's sunlight, of course. We use all kinds of lamps and light bulbs for light on cloudy days or in the evening. At night we sometimes see the light from the moon or the stars.

Take a moment to think about light. What do you already know about...

1. light sources and where you can find them?
2. what happens to light when it shines on different kinds of materials?
3. how shadows form?
4. mirrors and how they affect the direction of light?
5. the way objects can look in mirrors?
6. what happens to light when it travels through clear, colourless objects?
7. the colours of the rainbow?

What else would you like to discover about light?

Write your answers in your science journal. Don't worry if you can't think of some of the answers right now. In this unit you will discover new things about light to add to what you already know.

Looking for Light Sources

▲ When night falls, and the sun disappears, our world is plunged into darkness. It's no surprise, then, that we have always been interested in finding ways to light up the night.

A light source is the place or object that light comes from. We use many different light sources. You have probably used a few light sources already today.

In **Getting Started** you will compare the light sources of 100 years ago with the light sources we use today. In **Let's Investigate** you will list and sort the light sources in your home. In **Investigating Further** you can research where the fuel for artificial light sources comes from.

GETTING STARTED

How many light sources can you find in each picture on page 140? Explain how the light from each light source is created. How are the light sources in the pioneer room different from the ones you use today?

LET'S INVESTIGATE

Be on the lookout for light sources! What light sources can you find at home?

1. Choose a room in your home.

2. Be on the lookout for light sources! Look for any places or objects that light is coming from.

3. Write the name of the room in your science journal. Underneath it, list all the light sources you observed.

4. Move to another room. Be on the lookout for more light sources. Write the name of this room in your science journal. Then list all the light sources you find.

5. Keep hunting through every room in your home until you think you've found all the light sources.

List all possible light sources, even if they aren't on while you're looking. For example, a bedroom lamp is still a light source, whether it's on or off.

Reflect on Your Results

1. Organize the results of your light-source hunt. Sort your light sources into two groups. Use the headings Natural Light Sources and Artificial Light Sources for the two groups.

2. Explain the purpose of each artificial light source. In other words, why did someone invent it?

Natural light comes from natural sources, such as the sun. Artificial light comes from sources that people have made, such as a light bulb.

Light Bulbs

You probably noticed that light bulbs give off a lot of heat. In fact, many light sources give off heat. The sun does. So does a candle. So does an electric stove element.

Heat and light are related. They're both kinds of energy. There are other kinds of energy, too. The Soundscapes unit in this book is all about another kind of energy: sound.

Energy can be changed from one form to another. For example, electrical energy can be changed to light energy. This happens naturally with lightning. Most of the light sources you depend on, however, are artificial light sources that use electricity. All the light bulbs that light up your life at school, at home, in stores, and on streets at night run on electricity.

Most light bulbs waste a lot of electricity. That's because they give off so much heat. In fact, nearly all the electricity that goes into these light bulbs winds up becoming heat. Only a bit of it is changed to light energy. Why do we use light bulbs, then? They're pretty cheap to buy, and they've been around for a long time—more than 100 years. Old habits are hard to break!

There are some alternatives to light bulbs, however. For example, the lights above you right now are probably fluorescent light tubes. These lights give off some heat, but much less than ordinary light bulbs do. They also last much longer. Less heat and longer life mean they waste less electricity.

How do fluorescent light tubes work? There's a gas inside the tubes. When electricity runs through this gas, it gives off a kind of light that people can't see. It's called ultraviolet light. The insides of the tubes are coated with something that glows when it's hit by this invisible light. That glow is what lights up a room when fluorescent lights are turned on.

These photos show some other light bulbs that work in the same way that fluorescent lights do.

What Did You Learn?

1. Identify the light source in each photo as natural or artificial. Give reasons for your answers.

2. Why do you think people have invented so many different ways to make light?

3. Here are some examples of artificial light sources. Create a timeline for these light sources. Order them from the oldest to the most modern.

   candle

   light bulb

   fluorescent light tube

   torch

   oil lamp

   lantern

   lighthouse

INVESTIGATING FURTHER

Researching Fuel Sources for Light

All artificial light sources need electricity or another fuel to run. What kinds of fuels have people used to create light through history? Where did they find the fuels? Use reference materials or the Internet to find the answers. Make a poster to present your research.

Some natural light sources are animals! This picture shows fireflies lighting up the night. What other animals make their own light?

Shine On

So far in this unit, you've been looking for light sources. Now that you've found them, it's time to get rid of them—well, a few at least! In Getting Started you will use what you know about light to make your classroom as dark as possible. In Let's Experiment you will test materials to see how much light they let through. In Investigating Further you can change your experiment to learn more about light.

GETTING STARTED

Brainstorm with your class all the ways you can think of to make your classroom as dark as possible. These questions can give you some ideas:

- What kinds of light sources are lighting up your classroom?
- Does the light from each source spread in all directions, or is it only directed in one direction?
- Which light sources can be turned off?
- Which light sources can be removed?
- What else can you do?

Use the ideas from your brainstorming to develop a plan and carry it out.

How dark can you make your classroom?

LET'S EXPERIMENT

What types of materials are best for keeping light out? Which materials let light through easily? This activity will help you explore these questions.

1. Make a chart like this in your science journal. Use it to record all your observations.

Material	How much light shines through?			Do you notice anything else?
	Lots	Some	None	

You will need
- a flashlight
- different kinds of paper (such as writing paper, newspaper, tissue paper)
- different kinds of food wraps (such as plastic wrap, aluminum foil, waxed paper)
- different kinds of fabric (such as cheesecloth, wool, nylon)

2. You will be given a box that contains a flashlight and different kinds of materials. Remove everything from the box.

3. Ask each person in your group to choose a role. The roles are
- flashlight operator
- material holder
- observer
- recorder

4. When the lights are turned off, it's time to start. Choose one material from the box. Turn on the flashlight, and point it at the material. Record your observations.

5. Change roles with the members in your group. Choose another material, and repeat steps 4 and 5 until you've tested all the materials.

Reflect on Your Results

1. Which materials let all of the light pass through?

2. Which materials let none of the light pass through?

3. Which materials let some of the light pass through?

4. Read the Information Station to learn how scientists describe the effects you've just observed.

What Happens When Light Shines on a Material?

Some materials let light pass through them. Clear glass is an example of a material that light passes through easily. Clear glass and a clear sheet of ice let light pass through in the same way. Scientists use the word **transparent** to describe these materials. All transparent materials let light pass through them.

Other materials block light from passing through. When light shines on them, none of the light passes through. A wooden door is an example of a material that blocks light. Wood, carpeting, and even most parts of your body block light. Scientists use the word **opaque** to describe these materials. All opaque materials block light from passing through them.

Some materials block some light that shines on them, but also let some of the light pass through. Waxed paper and frosted glass are two examples. Scientists use the word **translucent** to describe these materials. All translucent materials let some, but not all, light pass through them.

▲ Some light bulbs, like this frosted one, are made so that the light they give off is softer. The glass is made with a translucent material that lets only some light pass through.

▲ This window is made of transparent glass, so that light can pass through it.

▲ This wooden door is opaque. It blocks light from passing through it.

What Did You Learn?

Look at the materials you tested in this activity.

1. Name two opaque materials. How do you know they're opaque?

2. Name two translucent materials. How do you know they're translucent?

3. Name two transparent materials. How do you know they're transparent?

4. How could you turn a translucent material into an opaque material?

5. How could you turn an opaque material into a translucent material?

6. Review your plan for making your classroom dark. What changes, if any, would you make to your plan? Explain your reasons.

Add the words **transparent**, **opaque**, and **translucent** to your science journal. Write the meaning of each in your own words, and then use each in a sentence.

Every time you see a word in **bold** type throughout this unit, repeat this step.

INVESTIGATING FURTHER

Making Predictions

Predict the results of your activity if you used a different light source.

Predict the results of your activity if you moved the light source closer to the material.

What would happen if the light source was moved farther away? Make a prediction and then test it.

Shadowplay

Each of these children has a shadow. When have you noticed shadows? In **Getting Started** you will discuss what causes shadows. In **Let's Experiment** you will make shadows and test some statements about shadows. In **Investigating Further** you can learn about shadow plays.

GETTING STARTED

What type of a day does it have to be to see shadows? Discuss in class what you think causes shadows. Share your answers. What do you agree about? What, if anything, do you disagree about?

LET'S EXPERIMENT

Get ready to test some ideas about light.

1. In this activity you will design your own experiments to test the following statements.

   True or False?

   a) Shadows are made whenever an object blocks light from a light source.

   b) Shadows get bigger when the object is farther away from the light source.

   c) Shadows get smaller when the object is closer to the light source.

   d) Shadows are very crisp and clear when the object is closer to the light source.

   e) Shadows are hazy and blurry when the object is farther from the light source.

   f) Opaque objects are best for making shadows.

   g) Translucent objects are best for making shadows.

   h) Transparent objects are best for making shadows.

   i) Shadows stay where they are, no matter where the light source is.

   j) An object can have more than one shadow.

2. There are many statements to design tests for. Discuss with your class how to organize and share all the tasks. You may also ask your teacher for help.

You will need
- a flashlight
- two opaque materials
- two translucent materials
- two transparent materials
- a wall or screen to observe shadows

TIP

Each of these statements may or may not be true. That's why the tests you design are important. They will help you decide whether the statements are true.

3. Think about how you will record your observations in your science journal. You may find it helpful to create a chart, or you might prefer to draw sketches showing the positions of the light source, the wall, and the object you're testing.

4. When you're ready to begin your tests, ask your teacher to turn off the lights. Then play with the shadows.

5. When you have finished your tests, ask your teacher to turn on the lights. Record your observations in your science journal.

Reflect on Your Results

Review your answers to the questions about shadows.

1. How did the flashlight help you when answering the questions?

2. You used three different types of materials: opaque, translucent, and transparent. Describe the shadows made by each type of material.

3. Explain your methods for discovering whether an object can have more than one shadow.

What Did You Learn?

1. Explain which type of material is the best for making shadows: opaque, transparent, or translucent?

2. Look at pictures A, B, C, and D on this page and on page 154. Predict what the shadows will look like in each picture. Describe where the shadow will appear, and its shape and size.

3. Look at pictures A and B. In which picture would the shadow be the largest?

4. Look at pictures C and D. In which picture would the shadow appear above the ball? below the ball?

▲ Picture A

▲ Picture B

(Please see next page.)

▲ Picture C

▲ Picture D

This is a photo of a lunar eclipse. Lunar means moon, and eclipse means darkening. So a lunar eclipse is a darkening of the moon. If you think that means there's a shadow involved, you're right! It's a shadow of the planet earth on the moon. In a lunar eclipse the earth passes between the sun and the moon and a shadow of the earth is cast on the moon.

INFORMATION STATION

Thousands of years ago people noticed objects and the shadows they cast. They saw the lengths of the shadows change with the time of day. Shadows became shorter at noon and longer in the evening. Look at these two pictures. See the difference when the sun is overhead at noon and when it is lower later in the afternoon.

Use library books or the Internet to find out more about shadow plays.

▲ shadows at noon   ▲ shadows in late afternoon

When people looked at the sun thousands of years ago, they discovered they could use shadows to tell time. They even invented an instrument for telling time using the position of a shadow cast by the sun. Sundials are found in parks and even in some people's gardens. The earliest sundial was found in Egypt and dates from about 3500 years ago.

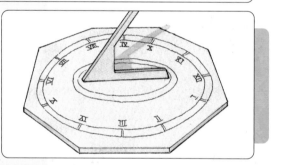

INVESTIGATING FURTHER

Researching Shadow Plays

Many Asian cultures have a long tradition of using shadows and puppets to put on dramatic performances. These "shadow plays" are common in China, Thailand, and Indonesia. Find out about this art. How are the puppets made? How are shadow plays put on? You might try putting on a shadow play with some classmates.

Mirror Images

Light reflects in different ways off many surfaces. We use many tools that do their job by reflecting light. In **Getting Started** you will decide what kind of surface makes the clearest reflection. In **Let's Experiment** you will discover what happens to light that reflects in a mirror.

GETTING STARTED

If you wanted to look at yourself, which one of the items on page 156 would you use? Which one would let you see yourself best? Which ones wouldn't be as good? If you were going to design a device for looking at yourself, what features would it have? Why?

LET'S EXPERIMENT

How can light change direction? This activity will help you find out for yourself.

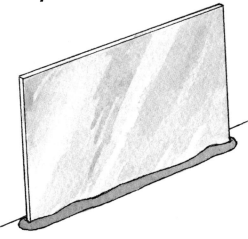

You will need
- a mirror
- a flashlight
- modelling clay (to keep mirror standing up)

1. Put a strip of modelling clay along one edge of a mirror. Then stand the mirror upright.

2. Stand directly in front of the mirror. Then take two side steps to your left. Turn your body so you're facing the centre of the mirror. (See the picture on page 158.)

3. When everyone is ready, your teacher will turn off the lights.

4. Turn on the flashlight and shine a beam of light at the mirror. What happens to the beam of light?

5. Stand directly in front of the mirror again. Then take two steps to your right. Turn your body so you're facing the centre of the mirror, and shine a beam of light at it. What happens to the beam of light? (Please see next page.)

Be very careful when you are handling and working with mirrors. Some are made of glass. They break easily and have sharp edges.

6. Hold the flashlight above your head and then at knee level, and shine the light at the mirror each time. What happens to the beam of light each time?

7. Let everyone in your group take turns using the flashlight, and repeat steps 2 to 6.

8. Choose a spot behind you in the classroom. This is your target. Figure out where you have to stand so that you can shine a beam of light at the mirror and hit the target.

9. Choose a new target, and let someone else try to hit it with a beam of light.

10. When the lights have been turned on again, record your results in your science journal.

Reflect on Your Results

You've just been experimenting with a property or feature of light. It's called **reflection**. Discuss with your class a definition for reflection.

Compare your group's definition with one found in a dictionary.

What Did You Learn?

1. What will happen to the beam of light in each of the cases on this and on the next page?

(Please see next page.)

2. When scientists study light, they often need to describe the path that light follows when it travels from a light source. Scientists say that light follows a straight-line path. In other words, light travels in a straight line. What proof have you seen of light travelling in a straight line? Give an example.

Mirror, Mirror

It's hard to say when people first realized that they could use the surface of water as a mirror. Certainly, it must have been a very long time ago.

And we don't know when people began making mirrors. It was at least 5000 years ago. We know this because archeologists—scientists who explore our past— have discovered metal mirrors in Egypt that date from that time period.

Most mirrors that we know about were made of shiny, polished metal until about 700 years ago. That's when glass mirrors, like the kind you have at home, became popular.

Believe it or not, glass mirrors still have metal in them. Mirrors are made out of very smooth glass. One side is coated with metal—often either silver or aluminum. The glass is transparent. It lets light travel through it easily. When light strikes the metal layer, it reflects off it.

More With Mirrors

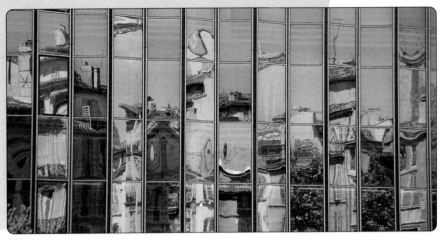

▲ Do these buildings really look like this?

▲ Did someone make a mistake with this word?

▲ Can this little wire really let you talk on the phone and surf the Internet?

Believe it or not, all of these questions have something in common. All of them depend on the ability of light to reflect from mirrors.

In Getting Started you will recall and classify mirrors you have seen recently. In Let's Investigate you will investigate some properties of reflections. In Investigating Further you can learn how magicians use mirrors to perform their tricks.

GETTING STARTED

How many mirrors have you seen during the past few days? Where did you see them? What are they used for? What other uses of mirrors do you know or can you think of?

LET'S INVESTIGATE

This activity will give you some more chances to reflect on different types of mirrors and how they reflect light.

STATION A: HOW MANY REFLECTIONS?

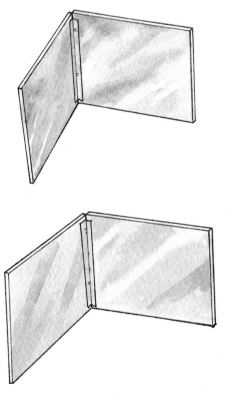

1. Notice the angle of the mirrors. When you are finished at this station, return the mirrors to this angle.

2. Place one of the objects between the two mirrors. How many reflections do you see? Record your observations in your science journal.

3. Carefully move the mirrors so that they're farther apart. How do the reflections change? Record your observations.

4. Carefully move the mirrors so that they're closer together. How do the reflections change? Record your observations.

5. Experiment with the other objects. Note how their reflections change in all cases. Record your observations.

6. Return the mirrors to their original angle.

You will need
- for station A: two mirrors taped together and a few small objects such as a pencil and an eraser
- for station B: two mirrors and a few small objects such as a pencil and a glue bottle
- for station C: a mirror, small pieces of paper, and a pen or pencil
- for station D: a clean metal spoon

Be very careful when you are handling and working with mirrors. Some are made of glass. They break easily and have sharp edges.

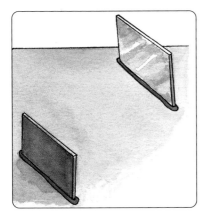

STATION B: COUNT THESE REFLECTIONS (IF YOU CAN!)

1. Place one of the objects between the two mirrors. What do you see? Record your observations.

2. Remove the object. Repeat step 1 using other objects. Also try placing them closer to one mirror than to the other. What do you see in each case? Record your observations.

Writing a mirror-message can be trickier than you might expect. How might you make it simpler?

STATION C: CATCHING A CODE

1. Write a short message on a piece of paper. Hold it up so that it is facing the mirror. What happens to your message?

2. Now write a mirror-message to a member of your family. In other words, write the message so that it looks like secret writing if you're just looking at it, but it looks normal when you look at its reflection. When you get home, your family member will have to figure out how to decode your message!

STATION D: DISTORTING REALITY (CURVED MIRRORS)

1. Hold up a shiny metal spoon so that the inside part—the bowl of the spoon—is facing you. In your science journal, describe your reflection.

2. Turn the spoon around so that you're looking at the bottom of it. In your science journal, describe your reflection.

3. See what happens when you try to reflect light from each side of the spoon. Try different positions to see if you can control where the light reflects.

STATION E: LIGHT RELAY CHALLENGE

1. You already know that light travels in straight lines. This means, then, that you can't shine a beam of light around a corner, right? Or can you? How?

2. Here's your challenge: Send a beam of light out of your classroom so that it shines on an object that is around a corner.

Brainstorm different ways to do it. Decide what you'll need to do it. Then do it!

Reflect on Your Results

1. Which will show more reflections: picture 1 or picture 2? Can you explain why?

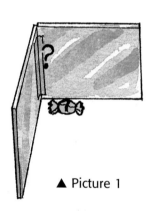

▲ Picture 1

▲ Picture 2

2. Schrine looked at herself in a mirror. She raised her right hand, and when she looked in the mirror it looked as if she had raised her left hand. How is this similar to your mirror-message in station C?

3. Which of these sentences best describes how you look when you observe your reflection in a spoon:
   - I look like I do when I look at myself in a flat mirror.
   - I look distorted.
   Why do you think you look that way?

4. Light travels in a straight line. How were you able to make a beam of light go out of your classroom door and around a corner?

The ability of light to reflect from mirrors plays an important role in our lives. Here are just a few examples.

The curved surface of this mirror lets drivers see more area to the side of their vehicles.

Flashlights have a curved mirror surrounding the little light bulb. It helps collect the light that travels from the bulb and send it out in one direction.

Dentists rely on tiny mirrors to help them get the best possible look at your teeth. Imagine how difficult their job would be without these little reflectors!

In station E: Light Relay Challenge, you were able to make light follow a crooked path, even though light can only travel in straight lines. The wire you see in the picture at the bottom of the page can help light do the same thing. It's called an optical fibre, and it's only about as thick as a strand of hair on your head. Optical fibres are made of glass or plastic. Their smooth surfaces are designed to reflect highly focused light called laser light. Optical fibres can be used to carry information in the form of light signals, much as telephone wires and television cables carry information in the form of electrical signals. Although electricity and light travel at the same speed, the optical fibres carry thousands of times more information than wires of the same size can carry.

What Did You Learn?

This is called a "solar furnace" or a "solar cooker". It uses the sun to cook food. Look at the picture closely. What do you notice? How do you think it works?

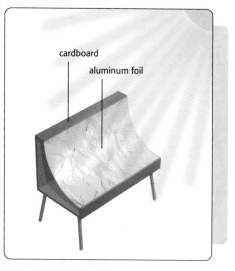

cardboard

aluminum foil

INVESTIGATING FURTHER

Creating Illusions

How are mirrors used in magic shows? Magicians prefer to be called illusionists and depend on mirrors for some of their illusions. Find out what kinds of effects mirrors help them create. (Be forewarned, though. Illusionists like to guard their tricks and secrets carefully. You may need to pull out a few tricks of your own to get them to share what they know!)

Lenses

You've probably seen or used most of these inventions. Many of them play a role in your daily life. Believe it or not, only one of these inventions is very modern. It was invented in the early 1980s. All the others are at least 100 years old. Some of them are much, much older. Try to figure out the timeline-sequence for these inventions.

What does any of this have to do with light? All of these inventions use the same kind of device to make light change direction. It's called a lens.

In **Getting Started** you will examine some examples of lenses at work. In **Let's Observe** you will make your own magnifier. In **Investigating Further** you can discover how people in your community use lenses.

GETTING STARTED

A lens is made of transparent material. Lenses are usually made of glass or plastic. In nature, lenses can be made of any transparent material. There are natural lenses in our eyes and the eyes of other animals. Where else in nature might you find a lens?

What do you think is going on in these pictures? Ask your teacher for materials that will let you try these situations out for yourself. Try to figure out what's happening, or why.

▲ Is this pencil really bent?

▲ Does this person really have such short legs?

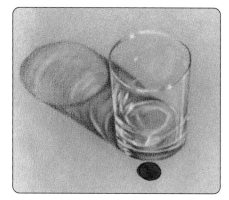

▲ In this picture, you can't see anything in the glass.

▲ Water has been poured into the glass. Was the penny really there all the time?

What Happens When Light Shines on a Material?

Light travels amazingly fast. Snap your fingers. In the time it takes to snap your fingers, light can travel around the earth about seven times. That's really fast!

When a beam of light travels from one transparent material, like air, into another transparent material, like water, light slows down. This slowdown causes light to change direction.

This is similar to what would happen if you pushed a wagon along a sidewalk and slowly edged it toward the grass that runs beside the sidewalk. The grass is harder for the wagon to roll on. If you push the wagon in a straight line and gradually move toward the grass, the wheels that roll onto the grass first will slow down and make the wagon move slightly off its straight-line path. Then it will travel on a new straight-line path.

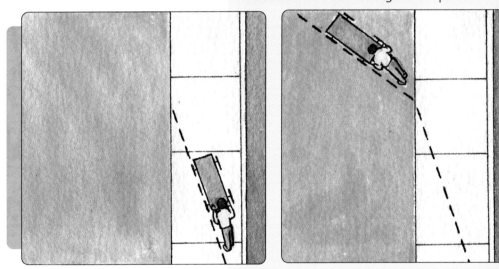

When light changes direction like this, some interesting effects can happen. All the effects shown in Getting Started are caused by this change of direction. In the next activity, you'll observe some other effects.

LET'S OBSERVE

Use water to make a big difference in the way you look at things!

PART 1: LOOKING THROUGH WATER DROPS

1. Put a rectangle of clear plastic on a small piece of newspaper. Use your finger to place a small drop of water onto the plastic. Keep the drop of water as small as possible. If you can get it to be about the size of the tip of your pencil, that's great.

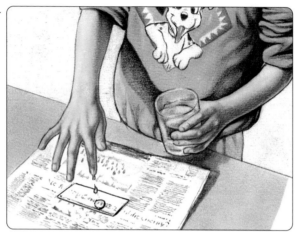

2. Look through your water drop from directly above. Record your observations.

3. Slowly and carefully lift the plastic rectangle off the paper, but keep looking through the drop of water. Record your observations.

4. Make a new water drop near your first one. Make the new one larger—about twice the size of the first. Look at another part of the newspaper through the new drop of water. Then slowly and carefully lift the rectangle off the paper, and look through the large drop of water. Record your observations.

5. Look at the water drop from a side view, and sketch what you see.

6. Use a magnifying glass, and look at the newspaper. Sketch what you see.

You will need
- small, clear plastic rectangles, some newspaper, and water
- a small plastic transparent container with lid, some newspaper, and water
- small pieces of newspaper or magazines
- a small, clear jar
- a magnifying glass

To learn how to make another kind of magnifier, see the Toolkit on page 245.

PART 2: LOOKING THROUGH A JAR

1. Fill your jar completely full with water. Put the lid on tightly.

2. Turn the jar on its side, and roll it onto a piece of newspaper. Look at the newspaper through your jar. Look from different angles. Record your observations.

3. Hold the jar at eye level, and look at your classmates through it. Ask them what they see when they look at you.

4. Sketch the shape of the jar the way it looks from the side as it's lying on the newspaper.

5. Use a magnifying glass to look at the newspaper and your classmates. Record your observations.

Reflect on Your Results

1. Compare your two drops of water. Which one worked better: the smaller drop or the larger one? Can you explain why?

2. Compare your drops of water with the clear jar. Which one worked better, in your opinion?

3. Is the magnifying glass more like the water drops or the jar?

4. The magnifying glass is an example of a lens. The water drops and your jar acted like lenses, too. The word *lens* comes from an ancient word for a type of seed called a lentil. Here are some lentils. What do you notice about their shape? Try to figure out how lenses got their name.

5. Read Scientists in Action to find out about a scientist who was an expert at making magnifying lenses.

SCIENTISTS IN ACTION

Antony van Leeuwenhoek and His Amazing Magnifiers

Nobody knows when people first started making lenses. It is believed that water-filled glass balls were used as lenses about 2000 years ago. (They acted like your water-filled jar.) About 1000 years ago or earlier, similar lenses were probably used by explorers from the Middle East. About 700 years ago, people were making lenses in Europe.

One of history's best lens makers was a man from the Netherlands named Antony van Leeuwenhoek. (His name is pronounced LAY-vun-hook.) He lived a long life, from 1632 to 1723, and made several contributions to science.

Leeuwenhoek possessed three valuable skills that all good scientists share: patience, the ability to make keen observations, and a desire to share his discoveries with the rest of the world.

What did Leeuwenhoek do? He made lenses better than anyone else did. Actually, his lenses continue to amaze scientists even today. It wasn't until the late 1800s that people developed the knowledge and the technology to improve on his lenses.

No one knows when Leeuwenhoek first began making lenses or when he started using them to make tiny things look bigger. The first time the world heard about him was in 1673. That's when he wrote a long report to a major scientific group in England called The Royal Society. In this and other reports, Leeuwenhoek wrote about the tiny living things he discovered in pond water. Today, we have names for these tiny living things. But back then, nobody had ever seen them before. That's because they are invisible to the eye unless you have a strong magnifying lens.

By the time of his death, Leeuwenhoek had made more than 400 lenses. All of them were quite small. Most were about the size of a water drop. His smallest lens was made from a single grain of sand!

These living things are found in water all over the planet. Unless you have a magnifying lens, they're invisible to you. ▼

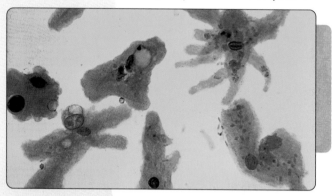

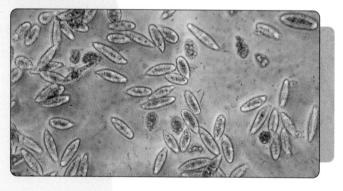

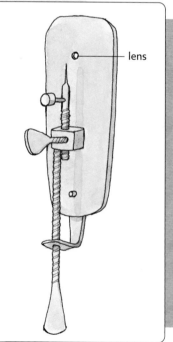

lens

◀ Leeuwenhoek's microscope

If you want to learn more about Leeuwenhoek and his magnifying lenses, look for this book:

Antoni Van Leeuwenhoek: First to See Microscopic Life
by Lisa Yount in **Great Minds of Science series** (Enslow Publishers: Springfield, New Jersey, U.S., 1996). (Don't worry about "Antony" being spelled "Antoni". There are different ways of spelling his name.)

What Did You Learn?

1. Leeuwenhoek worked for many years to understand how to make good lenses. What does that tell you about him as a scientist?

2. Someone who needs glasses to read small print has forgotten them. What could he or she do to read a telephone number?

INVESTIGATING FURTHER

How Do We Use Lenses?

Conduct a survey of businesses in your community. Find out who uses lenses and what they're used for. Also ask what training the people have had to help them use lenses in their work.

The Colours of the Rainbow

A rainbow is one of nature's most beautiful spectacles. When sunlight passes into and out of raindrops, a rainbow forms in the sky. Sunlight has travelled through nature's lenses: raindrops.

In Getting Started you will begin to hypothesize, or predict, how white light from the sun makes rainbows. In Let's Observe you will use lenses or prisms to make your own rainbows. In Investigating Further you can learn about other kinds of energy that are similar to light energy.

GETTING STARTED

A rainbow tells us something important about light. Find out for yourself what this is. Start by making a cardboard circle.

Use your ruler to draw a straight line across the middle of the circle. Then draw two more lines to form an X.

Your circle is now divided into six sections. Make each section a different colour of the rainbow. Colour one section red, another orange, yellow, green, blue, and purple.

Sharpen a pencil and carefully poke it through the centre of your circle. (That's the place where the three lines you drew all cross each other.) Then spin it like a top. What do you see?

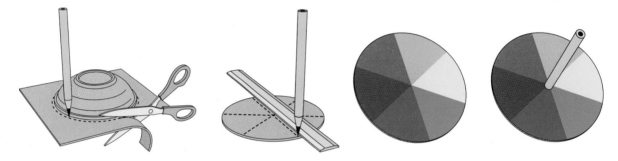

LET'S OBSERVE

You will need
- a prism
- water and some transparent containers to make homemade prisms
- a light source such as the sun, a strong flashlight, or a slide projector
- a white sheet of paper

A prism is a special kind of lens. Prisms come in different shapes, but you'll probably see them mainly in the shape of a triangle. In this activity, you'll use prisms to make rainbows.

1. Fill a glass about half way with water. You have just made a homemade prism! Choose other transparent containers, and make some more prisms.

2. Choose a prism. Try to get it to make a rainbow by putting it in front of a light source. In your science journal, describe how you did it and the colours you saw. If you can't make a rainbow, talk it over with other students and try to come up with a solution.

3. Repeat steps 1 and 2 for the rest of the prisms.

Reflect on Your Results

1. What colours did you observe using your first prism?

2. What colours did you observe using the rest of your prisms?

3. What did you notice about the pattern—the arrangement—of colours?

4. How did the colours you observed compare to the colours in a rainbow? Try to suggest a reason why.

5. Read the Information Station to learn more about the rainbow effect you've been observing.

A light box helps you shine a very thin beam of light on something. To learn how to make a light box, see the Toolkit on page 244.

INFORMATION STATION

Light Is a Mixture

Light from the sun usually looks somewhat white. Light from light bulbs often looks that way too. Scientists actually call this white light.

In 1666, one of the greatest scientists of all time, Isaac Newton, discovered that the sun's white light is really a mixture of different colours. It's a mixture of all the colours in the rainbow.

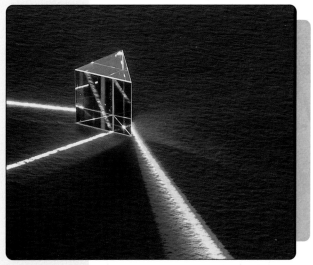

Newton repeated the same experiment that many scientists had already done and made sunlight travel through a prism. He saw exactly what you saw—all the colours of the rainbow. Then he made the light from the rainbow travel through another prism. What do you think he saw? He saw white light again. As a result of this observation, Newton concluded that white light is a mixture of colours. The first prism he used broke up the white light so he could see the colours. The second prism mixed it together again.

The bands of colour that form when white light passes through a prism are called a **spectrum**. The colours are always the same and they're always in the same order. They're red, orange, yellow, green, blue, and purple.

What Did You Learn?

1. What is a prism?

2. Explain how fresh, clear ice could be a prism.

3. What happens when sunlight travels through a prism? Use the term "transparent material" in your answer.

4. Explain why you might or might not consider a rainbow a spectrum.

INVESTIGATING FURTHER

If you want to do some more colour-related experiments for yourself, look for this book:
See Hear
by Milan Tytla (Annick Press: Toronto, ON, 1994). Be sure to check out page 91 for an experiment that will let you watch water flow backwards, back into the faucet!

Other Kinds of Energy

In Getting Started, you spun colours around. The result was close to white. However, if you take red paint or a red crayon and mix it with orange, yellow, green, blue, and purple paints or crayons, you won't get white. You'll get, well, try it and find out. Afterwards, do some research to find out why you got the result that you did.

The spectrum of white light is really only a small part of a much broader spectrum of energy that light is a part of. This broader spectrum of energy includes heat energy. Light and heat are closely related. The broader spectrum of energy also includes ultraviolet energy. It's sometimes called UV or UV radiation. You've probably heard about health warnings connected to ultraviolet energy. Why are scientists so concerned about it? What can this energy do to you? What precautions can you take to stay safe and healthy?

Show What You Know About Light

Light is important in all our lives. Why is it important in your life? These pictures show a few possibilities that might apply to you. What others can you think of?

In **Getting Started** you will develop lists of devices that depend on light to work. In **Let's Investigate** you will choose a design and materials and build a periscope or kaleidoscope. In **Investigating Further** you can design and build other devices that depend on light.

GETTING STARTED

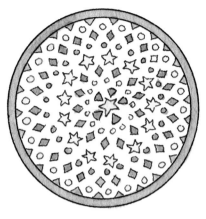

▲ This is an example of a kaleidoscope. The word *kaleidoscope* comes from three ancient words that mean "to look at pretty shapes".

Over the centuries, people have invented several devices that depend on light to work. Some of these devices are used to extend our sense of sight. A periscope is one example. The word *periscope* comes from two ancient words that mean "to look around".

What do you think a periscope is used for? What other devices can you think of that extend our sense of sight?

Some of these devices are used just for fun and amusement. A kaleidoscope (kah-LIE-doh-scope) is an example. What others can you think of?

LET'S INVESTIGATE

Be very careful when you are handling and working with mirrors. Some are made of glass. They break easily and have sharp edges.

You will need
● library books with instructions for making periscopes and kaleidoscopes

Build your own periscope or kaleidoscope.

1. Visit your school or local library. People have written many books about light. The library probably has a few of these books. Many books about light include instructions for making a periscope and a kaleidoscope.

2. Borrow a book from the library and bring it to class.

3. As a class, gather the periscope-making activities and kaleidoscope-making activities that were brought in. Decide how to share the resources so that everyone has instructions for building a periscope or a kaleidoscope.

4. Make sure your teacher approves of your activity. Decide how you'll obtain the materials and equipment you'll need. (If you get stuck, ask your teacher for some help.) Then start building!

1. Which learning events in this unit helped you make your periscope or kaleidoscope? How did they help?

2. How are periscopes useful? Who do you think uses them? Who do you think uses kaleidoscopes?

What Did You Learn?

1. At the beginning of this unit, you thought about several questions. You also jotted down your answers at that time. Look back at the questions and your answers. In your science journal, write at least two new things you learned in this unit and two things you already knew.

2. Scientists always have more questions than answers. What else would you like to learn about light?

INVESTIGATING FURTHER

Designing With Light

Here are several light activities that you might enjoy pursuing. Share your new discoveries with your class.

- Try making your own telescope or microscope. Keep journal entries describing how you made it, including sketches and labels. Let your classmates try it out, too!

- If you like taking photos, try making your own camera. It's easy, and you don't even need any fancy equipment. Look in a library book or in a database using the keywords *pinhole camera*. Other keywords you could try are *camera obscura*. Don't be put off by the weird name. It just means "darkened room".

- If you like taking photos, but aren't interested in building a camera, why not interview a photographer who takes photos for a living?

- Create a lighting plan for a two-storey house, without any use of electricity. Design the house, including all the rooms and where they are in the house. Your house can be a three-dimensional model or a two-dimensional drawing. This activity is a real challenge, but it can be lots of fun. See if anyone else in the class is interested, and work together as a team.

- One of light's "cousins"—the radio wave—has played a major role in letting people communicate. Find out what radio waves are and how they're related to light. Then research two pioneers in the field of using radio waves: the Italian technologist Guglielmo Marconi and the Canadian-born inventor Reginald Fessenden.

▲ telegraph

▲ 1930s radio

Thinking About Light Show

1. Name three natural light sources and three artificial light sources.

2. Draw yourself and your shadow at three different times of the day. Write the time under each drawing.

3. Give an example of an opaque, a translucent, and a transparent material. Which kind of material would you choose for bedroom curtains? Why?

4. Draw a diagram to show how light travels when it strikes a mirror.

5. Draw a picture or use words to explain how rainbows are made.

6. Which colours make white light?

7. Many devices depend on light to work. Name one that is very important to you. Describe how it uses light to work.

Earth Lab

Rocks are everywhere. Some lie buried so far underground that you'll never see them. Others stand so tall that their jagged peaks pierce the clouds.

Sometimes rocks hold treasures that sparkle in the sunlight. Sometimes they hide evidence of living things that grew or walked here millions of years ago.

What do you already know about...

1. the way rocks are formed?
2. the things rocks can tell us about the history of our planet earth?
3. the difference between rocks and minerals?
4. the forces that can wear down rocks —and the ways we try to stop those forces?
5. the things in your life that are made from rocks or minerals?

Write your answers to these questions in your science journal. When you finish this unit, look back at your answers. See how much you've learned about your world.

Rocks Everywhere

Have you thanked a rock today?

From the time you got up this morning, your life has revolved around rocks and materials that come from them. Think about what you've done so far today.

Have you
- looked out a window? Window glass is made from rocks.
- used any metal cutlery, like a spoon or fork? Metal comes from rocks.
- walked along a sidewalk? Sidewalks are made from rocks.
- opened a book? Paper is treated with materials that come from rocks.

In Getting Started you will collect rock samples. In Let's Observe you will examine your rocks and classify them. In Investigating Further you can imagine collecting rocks in space.

GETTING STARTED

To begin learning about rocks, collect three different kinds of rock. You may go out with your classmates to find them, or your teacher may ask you to collect them on your own and bring them to school.

Before you start, brainstorm as a class places that you think would be good for finding rocks. Discuss your ideas. How safe are these places? Do you need permission to go there? What will you need to take with you? When you go on trips like this, it's important to stay safe and to leave the place you're visiting the way you found it.

As a class, develop a set of safety guidelines to use when you collect your samples. Make sure everyone knows the guidelines. Then, go out and explore your planet earth!

If you are given permission to try to chip or break rocks with a chisel, protect yourself from flying pieces of rock. Wear protective goggles and cover the rock with a cloth first.

To learn how to make a simple magnifier, look in the Toolkit on page 245.

LET'S OBSERVE

What things make one rock different from another? What things do they have in common? Here's your chance to do some detective work and find out.

1. In a group, combine all of your rock samples.

2. Pick a rock from among these samples and examine it. Describe it in your science journal. Notice especially these kinds of details about it:
   - colour
   - texture (how it feels)
   - smell
   - weight (how light or heavy it feels)
   - anything else you find interesting

3. If you have a magnifier, use it to observe the rock. Add any new observations to your science journal.

4. Choose another rock to examine and describe.

5. Share your findings with the members of your group. Listen for the words that people use to describe the rocks.

You will need
- **your three rock samples**
- **a magnifier (optional)**

You may find it useful to set up a chart to organize your observations.

6. Classify all of your group's rock samples by sorting them into two or more piles. Write in your science journal how your group classified your rocks. When you're done, examine other groups' rock piles. Try to figure out what details they used to classify their rock samples.

Reflect on Your Results

1. In what ways are your group's rock samples different from each other?

2. In what ways are they similar to each other?

3. How did you use these similarities and differences to help you classify your rock samples?

4. Were you able to figure out the classification systems other groups used? If so, what helped you? If not, why did you have trouble?

You may want to compare the rock-collecting guidelines you wrote in Getting Started to the 10 rules in
Everybody Needs a Rock
by Byrd Baylor
(Macmillan/McGraw-Hill: New York, U.S., 1985).

What Did You Learn?

Imagine that one group of students classified their rocks by making four piles with three rocks in each pile. All the rocks in each pile looked so different that nobody in the class could figure out the group's classification system. So the group finally had to explain: "We classified the rocks by where we found them. Since we looked in four different places, we made four different piles."

What do you think of this classification system? Why? (Hint: First, think about why scientists and other people classify things.)

SCIENCE IN OUR LIVES

Calling All Rock Collectors!

People of all ages, all over the world, are fascinated by rocks. They like to go out hiking, trying to "sniff out" new rocks to add to their collections. Maybe that's why rock collectors prefer to be called by another name: rock hounds!

There are thousands of rock hounds in Canada. Some of them are professional scientists. Most, however, are "ordinary" people who love to observe or study rocks. Many of these people spend so much time with their rock-collecting hobby that they become experts at finding and identifying rocks.

Rock hounds often join rock clubs, which can be found in nearly every province across the country. There are more than 100 of them! These clubs hold meetings and set up shows so that rock hounds can get together. Members talk about their favourite collecting places, share stories, and trade rocks—just like other collectors trade stamps, cards, and comic books. Sometimes, rock clubs loan or donate rock samples to local museums.

Rock hounds are proud of the collections they put together, so they like to show them off. Small, shallow boxes make good display cases. They're also easy to store on bookshelves or in drawers. Each rock in the collection is labelled so that the "hound" knows where it came from, the date it was found, and what kind of rock it might be.

Why do you think people like to collect rocks? (If you're one of those people, why do you like it?)

Some rock hounds share their hobby on the Internet. To find them, try searching using "rocks or minerals".

INVESTIGATING FURTHER

Rock Collecting in Space

Rocks are everywhere on Earth—and beyond! Imagine what it would be like to go rock collecting on the Moon, on another planet such as Mars, or on an asteroid or comet. Write a story or draw a comic strip to describe your own off-world "hounding" adventure.

Minerals and Rocks

One of these two rocks could make you rich. The other would just look nice in your room. The top photo is of gold, one of the most valued natural materials in human history. The bottom photo is of pyrite, also known as "fool's gold". You can probably see the reason why! Actually, the two "rocks" in the photos aren't really rocks at all. They're minerals. The photos below show some other minerals. The photos on page 191 show some common rocks.

In Getting Started you will look at photos of minerals and rocks. In Let's Experiment you will compare rocks and minerals to identify them. In Investigating Further you can learn about a useful property of rocks and minerals.

GETTING STARTED

SOME COMMON MINERALS

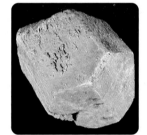

mineral 1 ▲

mineral 2 ▲

mineral 3 ▲

mineral 4 ▲

mineral 5 ▲

mineral 6 ▲

SOME COMMON ROCKS

rock 1 ▲

rock 2 ▲

rock 3 ▲

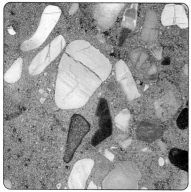

rock 4 ▲

rock 5 ▲

rock 6 ▲

rock 7 ▲

rock 8 ▲

rock 9 ▲

Very shortly you'll have a chance to touch and examine some **minerals** and rocks. So take some time to observe all the pictures closely. In your science journal, jot down any features that strike you about each mineral and each rock. If you really like any one mineral or rock, make a note of that too.

rock 10 ▲

LET'S EXPERIMENT

You will need
- a rock-and-mineral sample kit
- a magnifier

Use one full page in your science journal for each of the charts. Make sure you give yourself enough room to record your observations.

Some of the experiments that scientists do can be finished in a day or less. Others may take longer. (Some science experiments go on for years!) This activity is an experiment that may take longer than one day. That's because there's so much for you to do as you get to know more about minerals and rocks.

PART 1: OBSERVING ROCKS AND MINERALS

Can you tell the difference between a mineral and a rock? Look carefully, and you will begin to notice that minerals and rocks have different features.

1. Match each mineral and rock in your group's sample kit to one of the minerals and rocks in the photos on page 190 and page 191. Make two charts like the ones below in your science journal to record your matches. Use the rock and mineral samples from your kit to find the name of each rock and mineral in the photos. Complete the first and second column in each chart.

Mineral Number	Name of Mineral	Features I Observe
1		
2		
3		

Rock Number	Name of Rock	Features I Observe
1		
2		
3		

The photos and the items in your group's sample kit may not match up exactly. That's okay. See what clues you can use to help you make the match. If you're unsure about a decision, put a question mark beside the mineral or rock name you record.

2. Look at one of the rocks or minerals you like with the magnifier and then without it. Become as familiar as you can with the sample you're observing. Use the questions in the drawings below to help you. Record all your observations in the third column of the chart you started.

3. Repeat step 2 for each rock and each mineral.

4. You're now probably an expert at observing the features of your minerals and rocks. Use these features to sort all the samples in your group's kit into three piles.

Pile 1: Put all the samples that look like they're made up of only one big piece that's the same throughout in this pile.

Pile 2: Put all the samples that look like they're made up of two or more kinds of pieces stuck together in this pile. (The sizes of the pieces can be big enough to see without a magnifier or very tiny.)

Pile 3: This is your "We're not sure" pile. Put any samples you have difficulty sorting here.

Reflect on Your Results

1. Review what you recorded in column 1 and column 2 of your charts. Were you able to match all the samples from your kit to the examples in the pictures? If not, explain why you had difficulty. What other information would have helped you make the matches?

2. Did the magnifier help you make your observations? How? Would you have been able to make all your observations without it? Explain.

3. Look closely at the items you placed in the three piles. Take another look at pile 3 to see if you notice anything that can help you move a sample into pile 1 or pile 2. Then, visit other groups in the class to see how they sorted their piles. Maybe they can help you with your pile 3. Maybe you can help them with theirs. See if you can help your group and other groups get rid of pile 3 completely.

4. What is the same about all the samples in pile 1? What is the same about all the samples in pile 2?

Minerals are the same material throughout. Rocks are made of different materials (made up of small pieces of minerals) held together. Did you put all the minerals in pile 1 and all the rocks in pile 2? If you did, congratulations! If you didn't, don't worry. Even experienced rock (and mineral) hounds sometimes have trouble classifying some of the samples they find.

Use the pictures in this book and the charts you made to help you return each rock and mineral to its proper place in the kit.

PART 2: A PROPERTY OF MINERALS

The **property**, or feature, of minerals you are about to explore is hardness. You may have noticed it in part 1. Some minerals may feel harder than others to the touch, but how can you tell if they actually are? Get ready to find out.

Scientists have a clever way to compare the hardness of different minerals. They scratch them. Then, they use the results of this scratch test to create a list that ranks the minerals from softest to hardest. But why read about it? Do a mineral hardness scratch test for yourself!

You will need
- the minerals from your rock-and-mineral sample kit
- a piece of cardboard (to protect tabletops)
- your fingernail
- a copper penny
- a steel nail

1. Make a chart like this in your science journal. Use it to record your observations.

Mineral I Am Testing	Can My Fingernail Scratch It?	Can a Penny Scratch It?	Can a Steel Nail Scratch It?

2. Hold one of the minerals from your kit firmly on the piece of cardboard. Scratch the mineral gently with the edge of your fingernail. Did your fingernail leave a mark on it? Record your observations in your chart.

Handle the steel nail very carefully to avoid accidents.

3. Pick up the copper penny, and scratch your mineral again. Record your observations.

4. Pick up the steel nail. Carefully scratch your mineral again. Record your observations.

5. Repeat steps 2, 3, and 4 on each of the other minerals. Remember to record your observations.

Reflect on Your Results

You used three objects to perform the hardness scratch test. Now use your observations to make a list that ranks the minerals in order from softest to hardest.

1. Can you clearly identify the softest mineral sample you tested? If so, write its name at the top of a clean page in your science journal.

2. Can you clearly identify the hardest mineral sample you tested? If so, write its name at the bottom of the same page and go to question 3. If not, go to question 4.

3. Rank your remaining minerals. If you're unsure about where to put a mineral on your list, go to question 4.

4. Need some help? Did two or more of your minerals get scratched by the same object, and you can't decide which mineral is the harder one? Here's a trick scientists added to the mineral hardness scratch test. They use the minerals themselves to scratch each other! So if a mineral can be scratched by another mineral, then it is softer than the mineral that scratches it.

5. When you have finished ranking the minerals, compare your list with those of your classmates. Which minerals did everyone give the same ranking? What might explain any differences between lists?

What Did You Learn?

1. What is meant by a "property" of a material? Name all the properties of minerals you used in part 1 to sort your minerals from your rocks. Name the other property you used in part 2 to rank your minerals.

2. In part 1 of this activity, you were asked to match the pictures of rocks and minerals with the samples in your kit. Review the matches you made, and verify them. ("Verify" means to check whether something is correct.) How can your understanding of mineral properties help you verify the matches?

3. A group of scientists performed the mineral hardness scratch test on some mineral samples. Their results are shown below. Use these results to rank the minerals in order from softest to hardest.

Mineral Name	Results of Mineral Hardness Scratch Test
diamond	can't be scratched by a steel nail, but can scratch all the other mineral samples
graphite	can be scratched by a fingernail
gold	can be scratched by a copper penny and just barely by a fingernail
magnetite	can be scratched by a steel nail
pyrite	can be scratched by a steel nail, but not by a copper penny
talc	can be scratched easily by a fingernail
topaz	can't be scratched by a steel nail

4. A rock collector found a sample that looked like gold or pyrite. How could she use the mineral hardness scratch test to check which she had found?

5. The mineral hardness scratch test could be done with rocks. However, the results would not be very useful. Why?

Properties Scavenger Hunt

You can investigate another property of minerals. Believe it or not, they have many properties. Knowing these properties helps scientists classify them. (After all, with 2000 or so minerals, it helps to know how to tell them apart!) Properties can also help people decide which mineral (or rock) they can use for a specific purpose.

Go on a "properties scavenger hunt". List one property of minerals or rocks, and give three examples of minerals or rocks that have it. Then, for each rock or mineral, tell how that property might help people use it. You may need to do some research to learn what rocks and minerals can be used for.

The Salt of Our Earth

Many minerals have shapes like this:

These are just a few of the crystal shapes that minerals have.

In Getting Started you will examine salt crystals. In Let's Experiment you will grow salt crystals. In Investigating Further you can design a test to learn how salt crystals form at different temperatures.

GETTING STARTED

One of the minerals on page 190 was once worth its weight in gold. In fact, it was used just like money. In China, it was even used to make money.

Today, this mineral is still highly valued for its many uses. These include

- flavouring food
- keeping food from spoiling
- making medicines
- colouring clothing
- helping to keep roads safe to drive on in winter
- helping you get clean when you wash

Do you know what it is? Salt—the same kind that you have at home in your kitchen! To find out its mineral name, get a magnifier and look at some table salt. Then, use the charts you made when you were observing rocks and minerals to discover its name.

You will need

- table salt
- warm water
- 1-mL measuring spoon
- a cup or container
- a stir stick
- plastic spoons
- dark tape
- masking tape
- a paper plate or aluminum pie pan
- an aluminum tart cup or a jar lid
- a magnifier

You may find it helpful to make a list of all the jobs involved. Look for ways to group similar jobs together.

In this experiment you will grow your own salt crystals. It's simple to do. However, there's lots to do to set it up. If all the members of your group help, you can get everything done quickly and smoothly.

1. Read the whole activity first. Decide as a group what jobs need to be done. Then, volunteer to do one of them. Make sure everyone has at least one job to do.

2. Gather one spoon for each group member and a paper plate (or pie pan), dark tape, and masking tape. Then, set them up so that they look like this.

3. Carry the spoon-and-plate setup over to a place where it can sit undisturbed for a few days.

4. Pour some warm water into a cup or container until it's about half full. Add 1 mL of salt to the water using the measuring spoon. Stir the mixture using the stir stick until you can't see the salt (the salt dissolves in the water). Keep adding salt, 1 mL at a time, until no more salt will dissolve in the water—when a few tiny pieces of salt just sit at the bottom no matter how much you stir.

5. Slowly and carefully, pour some salt water into each spoon. Try to get each spoon about two-thirds full.

6. Line a tart cup or jar lid with dark tape, and fill it with the leftover salt water. Your teacher will collect any salt water left in your cup.

7. Predict what will happen to the salt water. Observe the contents of your spoon and tart cup or jar lid with and without the magnifier. Do this at least once a day for the next few days. Record what you see in your science journal.

Have you ever left a little bit of water in a glass at home? What happened to the water the next day? Was it all still there? Was some of it missing? Think about these questions. Then, answer this question in your science journal: What do you think will happen to the salt water over the next few days?

What Did You Learn?

1. Describe how the contents of your spoon changed. What is the solid material that formed in your spoon? How do you know?

2. This picture shows the shoreline around the Dead Sea in Israel, the saltiest body of water in the world. What do you notice about the shoreline? Suggest a possible reason for it.

3. Why might knowing about crystal shapes be useful to scientists? Why else might someone be interested in crystal shapes?

INVESTIGATING FURTHER

Trying Different Temperatures

Would your observations in the experiment have been different if you had left your spoonful of salt water in a much colder place? What if you had left it in a much warmer place? Design a fair test to find out what would have happened in either case.

Making Rock

▲ Surtsey, Iceland

The island in this photo was born in 1963 when an underwater volcano erupted. Jets of hot melted rock (lava) surged up through the water and high into the air. As the lava fell back into the water, it cooled quickly and turned to solid rock. For four years, lava continued to flow from the volcano on and off until the volcano finally exhausted itself. What it left was a brand-new rock formation—an island rising 150 m above sea level and covering an area of nearly three square kilometres.

Our planet earth is constantly making new rocks. Most of this rock making happens over a very long time, though. Rocks can also form in ways that don't involve volcanoes.

In Getting Started you will sort rocks by the material they are made of. In Let's Investigate you identify and describe rocks. In Investigating Further you can explore how rocks are used as building materials.

GETTING STARTED

Try to group the rocks in your sample kit by the kind of material of which they seem to be made. Compare your groupings with those of your classmates.

How Do Scientists Classify Rocks?

Scientists have developed a useful way to classify rocks based on the way that rocks form. Using this system, scientists divide rocks into three main groups or families.

Rocks That Are Formed by Fire

Deep below the earth's surface, it's so hot that rocks and minerals melt and stay liquid. Sometimes this melted rock and mineral mixture, or **magma**, pushes its way to the surface. That's what happens when volcanoes erupt.

When magma is exposed to cold water or air, it cools and hardens very quickly. This often results in very hard rock that breaks quite easily, just like glass. Because the magma cools so quickly, mineral crystals don't have time to form in it. Obsidian is formed this way.

Sometimes the magma has lots of steam and other gases mixed in with it. If this mixture cools and hardens very quickly, the result is rock that looks like a hard sponge. Pumice is formed this way. Its holes make pumice light enough to float on water—the only rock that can do this!

Most often, the magma never reaches the earth's surface. It stays underground, where it pushes into cracks and crevices. There, it cools and hardens very slowly giving crystals lots of time to form. Later, movements of the earth bring the rock up to the surface. Granite is formed this way. Granite has mineral crystals big enough for you to see. Some of these are feldspar, quartz, mica, and another mineral called hornblende.

Scientists call these three rocks—granite, pumice, and obsidian—**igneous rocks**. The word igneous means "formed from fire". Why is igneous a good family name for these rocks? ▶

pumice ▲

obsidian ▲

granite ▲

Rocks That Form in Layers

On the earth's surface, rocks are exposed to weather and other forces that wear them down and break them apart. Many of the broken-down pieces get carried away by rivers. Some of them dissolve in the water. Lighter pieces get carried away by the wind.

limestone ▲

conglomerate ▲

▲ shale

sandstone ▲

All of these pieces, called **sediment**, eventually settle in layers on the ground and at the bottom of lakes and oceans. Often bits of dead plants and animals settle along with them. Eventually, the weight pushing down on the lower layers is so great that these layers harden together.

When the sediments that harden together have fairly large pieces, it results in rocks like conglomerate. Conglomerate looks like a bunch of pebbles and large sand grains all cemented together. That's exactly what it is.

When the sediments that harden together have fairly small pieces, like grains of sand, the result is rocks like sandstone. Sandstone has a rough, gritty feel and—believe it or not—many tiny air spaces inside it, so water can seep through sandstone.

When the sediments that harden together have very, very small pieces, the result is rocks like shale. Shale is hardened clay or mud. The sediments that form shale are so fine that there are no spaces for air. This means that shale is fairly waterproof. ▶

When minerals dissolve in water and the water dries up, the minerals harden together to form rocks like limestone. Made up mainly of the mineral calcite, limestone is smooth and very strong and hard. Limestone can also be formed from the shells and skeletons of many water animals (like clams and sea snails), which contain calcite. Over time, piles of these shells and skeletons get cemented together to form limestone. You can often still see shells and skeleton bits in limestone formed this way!

Scientists call these four rocks—conglomerate, sandstone, shale, and limestone—**sedimentary rocks**. Why do you think they gave these rocks this family name?

Rocks That Change Their Identity

Most of the sedimentary and igneous rock on our planet lies below the surface. About 10 km down, it is quite hot and the weight of the rocks above presses down on the rocks here. Although this heat and pressure aren't enough to melt the rocks, they do make the rocks soft enough to behave like modelling clay—to bend and fold over. This changes the original rock. More crystals may form in it or larger ones may grow. Rock particles may also get squeezed closer together.

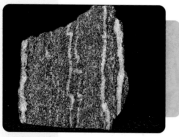

gneiss ▲

When all this "shape shifting" happens to granite, rocks like gneiss may form. Gneiss often has different-coloured stripes or bands that you can see without a magnifier.

When the shape shifting happens to shale, rocks like slate may form. Slate still has shale's waterproof property. Slate also splits easily into sheets, like the mineral mica. (In fact, mica is one of the minerals that make up slate.) School chalkboards are often made of slate.

slate ▲

When the shape shifting happens to a variety of different rocks and minerals, a rock like schist may form. There are many different types of schist because of the many different minerals it may contain.

schist ▲

Scientists call these three rocks—gneiss, slate, and schist—**metamorphic rocks**. The word metamorphic means "changed shape". Why is metamorphic a good family name for these rocks? (Metamorphic rocks can also change to form new metamorphic rocks.)

You will need
- reference books or CD-ROMs with information on rocks and minerals, or access to the Internet
- materials for making small posters

The special settings on a computer's word-processing program can help you make an eye-catching poster.

Help your classmates learn more about igneous, sedimentary, and metamorphic rocks.

1. Find a list of the names of the different kinds of rock in each family of rocks.

2. Choose one igneous, one sedimentary, and one metamorphic rock that was not in your sample kit.

3. Look up the following information about each of the rocks you've chosen:
   - what it's made of
   - how it forms
   - where you can find it (Can you find it near where you live? Why or why not?)
   - what properties it has that make it useful

4. Make a poster for each of your rocks that describes the rock but doesn't say which family the rock belongs to.

5. Trade posters with your classmates. See if they can figure out which rock is igneous, which sedimentary, and which metamorphic. Ask them what clues they used to decide.

What Did You Learn?

1. Make a chart that shows what the three rock families have in common and how they are different from each other.

2. Read Science in Our Lives. Why do you think Surtsey was protected so quickly and a rule made that only scientists could visit there?

3. Birds have been to Surtsey. So have seals. Do you think any other animals will ever live there permanently? Why or why not?

4. In what ways does this learning event show that scientists must be careful observers? patient? good record keepers?

SCIENCE IN OUR LIVES

Do you remember that new island, Surtsey? Even before it had finished forming, Surtsey was declared a nature preserve. Only scientists are allowed to visit it. That's because this new addition to our planet earth gives scientists a wonderful chance to observe how new life takes root on lifeless rock.

In 1975, a young science student named Borgthor Magnusson from Manitoba spent his summer on Surtsey. He has been returning there each year ever since.

Magnusson specializes in studying plants. He has set up a long-term project on Surtsey so that he and other scientists can observe which plants establish themselves on the island and how they do so.

Where would the plants come from, you might be wondering. Some seeds float there and the strong water current brings the seeds to the shore. That same water crashes against the shore, breaking parts of the shore down into small, sandy bits. Eventually, some seeds take root in the sandy soil formed this way.

Other seeds reach Surtsey carried by the wind and by birds that visit the island. So far, at least five different kinds of birds have set up permanent nesting spots on Surtsey. Many others stop there on their travels between Iceland and Europe.

INVESTIGATING FURTHER

Building With Rocks

Igneous, sedimentary, and metamorphic rocks play an important role in the paving of roads and the construction of buildings. Which rocks do we use for these construction projects? What properties make them useful in construction? How long ago do you think people discovered they could use them in these ways?

Explore an area of construction or architecture you find interesting. Find out how rocks are used in it. Then, decide how you can best share your discoveries with your classmates.

Our Ever-Changing Planet

Mighty forces are constantly at work reshaping our planet. Some of the resulting changes happen very slowly—so slowly that you could never hope to see them in your lifetime.

Other changes happen much more quickly. You may have seen the damage caused by an earthquake on TV or in a movie. Perhaps you've witnessed a flood or ice storm.

In Getting Started you will think about and imagine how natural forces affect the land. In Let's Experiment you will test how some natural forces affect sand and rock. In Investigating Further you can gather information about the Ice Age.

▲ Delicate Arch in Utah, United States

GETTING STARTED

The photos on this page show some examples of changes caused by natural forces. How do you think these formations were made? What forces were responsible? What might have happened to all the bits of rock that were carved away?

▲ hoodoos in Drumheller, Alberta

▲ The Rocks in New Brunswick

LET'S EXPERIMENT

Get ready to explore some of the forces that shape our planet—right in your own classroom!

STATION A: RAIN ON A SANDCASTLE

1. Let one person in your group make a sandcastle by filling the small container with damp sand and then overturning it onto the pie plate. In your science journal, make a sketch of your sandcastle in pencil. Add any labels you think are useful.

2. Fill a straw with water by placing one end in water and covering the other end with your fingertip or thumb. Then, lift the straw. Hold it about 15 cm above the top of your sandcastle, and drop the load of water. In your science journal, describe what happens to the sandcastle. On your sketch, record the changes that happen.

3. Take turns dropping 15 more straws full of water on the sandcastle, one at a time. After every 5 loads, describe what happens to the sandcastle and adjust your sketch to show the changes in your science journal.

You will need
- for Station A: a small plastic container, damp sand, an aluminum pie pan, a container of water, and a few plastic drinking straws that have been cut in half
- for Station B: a plastic jar with a lid; 5 to 10 small, clean stones; and water
- for Station C: Bag 1 and Bag 2 (prepared by your teacher)
- for Station D: same as for Station A, plus any other things you decide you need

STATION B: SHAKE, RATTLE, AND ROCK!

1. Put 5 to 10 small, clean rocks into a plastic jar.

2. Add water until the jar is about half full and put the lid on.

3. Now, shake it! Give the jar several hundred shakes. When you get tired, give the jar to another person in your group. Make sure everyone gets a turn.

4. Observe the contents of the jar closely. In your science journal, record everything you see.

STATION C: DEEP FREEZE

Your teacher soaked some rocks in water and put some of them into Bag 1 and some into Bag 2. Last night, your teacher put Bag 2 into the freezer and left it there until the rocks froze.

1. Observe and compare the contents of Bag 1 and Bag 2. In your science journal, record everything you see.

STATION D: SANDCASTLES—THE SEQUEL

1. You have already seen what happens to a sandcastle when it gets "rained on". Based on what you observed, think about these questions:

- What difference would it make if the sandcastle were taller or wider?
- What difference would it make if the sandcastle had a pointed top?
- What difference would it make if the straws full of water fell from higher up or lower down?
- What difference would it make if there were less water in each straw or more water in each straw?
- What difference would it make if you dropped fewer or more straws full of water on the sandcastle?

2. Choose one of these questions to follow up on. Predict what will happen. Then, design an experiment to test your predictions. Write down the steps you plan to follow. Show them to your teacher first. Then, try out your experiment.

3. If you like, choose another question from step 1 and repeat step 2.

Reflect on Your Results

1. What happened to your sandcastle at Station A? Where might this happen in nature? Explain.

2. What happened to the rocks at Station B? Where might this happen in nature? Explain.

3. What happened to the rocks at Station C? Where might this happen in nature? Explain.

4. How did your experiment or experiments at Station D turn out? How accurate were your predictions? If you were going to try one of your experiments again, what would you do differently?

5. Imagine that you built a mound of dirt one metre high in a protected area of your school yard (out of the wind). Describe how this mound might look one month later. Explain why any changes you described might happen.

INFORMATION STATION

Weathering and Erosion

Scientists often use the words **weathering** and **erosion** when they talk about the way changes happen to our planet earth. These words are so closely linked that they mean almost the same thing.

Weathering refers to all the ways that rocks can wear down and break into smaller pieces. Moving water can weather rock. Wind can, too. So can ice. What evidence have you seen that water, wind, and ice can weather rock?

Erosion refers to wearing away rock, too. But erosion has an added meaning. It also refers to what happens to the worn-down and broken bits of rock.

What does happen to them? Water, ice, and wind can carry pieces of rock to new places. In the activities you just finished, at which stations did you observe erosion? Where else have you noticed it?

The forces responsible for weathering and erosion can be very destructive. However, they are also very helpful. All the weathered and eroded bits of rock on our planet help form something in which your food grows: soil!

What Did You Learn?

1. This learning event is called Our Ever-Changing Planet. Is that a good title for it? If so, explain why. If not, explain why and suggest a better title.

2. In what way are the terms weathering and erosion similar? In what way are they different?

3. Water, wind, and ice can weather and erode rock. What other natural forces can weather and erode rock? Try to come up with at least two.

4. How do you think weathering and erosion help form soil? Why is this a good thing?

5. What did you do to make sure the experiments you designed were fair tests?

People Contribute to Weathering and Erosion, Too!

Here are some examples of the human activities that cause changes to our planet earth. Usually, we do these things for good reasons. Farming provides most of the food you eat. Cutting trees, or logging, provides most of the paper you use for writing on and for books. Digging up rocks, or mining, is the source of all the metal you use and of all the construction materials for the pavement and roads you travel on. You can probably think of many other examples.

However, we all pay a price for farming, logging, and mining. All of these activities open up the surface of the earth to the mighty forces of weathering and erosion. For example, when farmers plow their fields, they cut long grooves into the soil so that they can plant seeds. These grooves can collect water in a sudden or heavy rainfall. What might happen next? On the other hand, when there is no rain for a long time the plowed soil can dry out more quickly than soil that hasn't been plowed. In a strong windstorm, the dry, dusty soil can get picked up by the wind. What might happen next?

INVESTIGATING FURTHER

The Ice Age

If you had been alive 10 000 years ago, you would have had a tough time getting to school—or anywhere else for that matter. That's because a thick sheet of ice more than one kilometre deep covered much of Canada!

On the Internet or in the library, do a keyword search on the terms "glacier" and "Ice Age" to find out how moving rivers of ice have shaped the landscape of our country.

Can We Control Erosion?

If you'd like to read a story about how people's lives were affected by the Dust Bowl, look for this book:
The Dust Bowl by David Booth (Kids Can Press: Toronto, ON, 1996).

In the early 1930s, a severe drought ravaged the North American Prairies. The rich soil turned dry as dust. Then, violent windstorms pounded the Prairies. The dry soil, swept up by the winds, blanketed the sky with clouds of dust and dirt, making day like night.

Cattle and other livestock died by the thousands. Millions of people fled for their lives, and the wind carried tonnes and tonnes of topsoil far, far away.

Some good grew out of this "Dust Bowl". The farmers who came back learned new ways to protect their fields from wind erosion. The techniques they developed are still used today in Canada and around the world.

In **Getting Started** you will discuss the causes and effects of erosion. In **Let's Experiment** you will design a way of stopping water erosion. In **Investigating Further** you can use what you learned about preventing erosion to protect a sandcastle.

GETTING STARTED

Water erosion can damage farmers' fields just as easily, and as forcefully, as wind erosion can. Both water erosion and wind erosion can cause other dramatic landscape changes, too. What do you think caused the events in each of these pictures to happen? Who might have been affected by these events? How?

LET'S EXPERIMENT

People spend a lot of time in their gardens or on their farms trying to protect their soil from erosion. Work in a group to find out how well you can protect soil from erosion.

PART 1: WATCHING WATER FLOW

1. Lean one end of the piece of eavestrough against a support like a wall or one of the ladder rungs on a playground slide. See the illustration on page 216. Place the other end inside the collecting container.

2. Pour 1 L of water down the eavestrough. Estimate how long it takes for all the water to flow out. Record your estimate in your science journal.

3. Put enough soil into the eavestrough so that the soil is about 1 cm deep. Make sure you line the entire length of the eavestrough with soil. Now, set the eavestrough up exactly the way you did in step 1.

You will need
- for Part 1: 1 m of eavestrough; a clean, empty 1-L milk carton; water; soil; and a collecting container (such as a dishpan)
- for Part 2: the same materials as for Part 1, plus any additional materials you decide you need
- for Part 3: resource materials for research

4. Pour 1 L of water down the eavestrough again. Estimate how long it takes for all the water to flow out. Record what you observe.

Reflect on Your Results

1. Compare how long it took for the water to flow out of the eavestrough when it was empty (step 2) and when it had soil in it (step 4).

2. What else did you observe in step 4? Why do you think it happened?

PART 2: STOPPING WATER FROM FLOWING

1. Think about what you observed during step 4 in the first part of this activity. Brainstorm ideas and techniques to hold the soil in place.

2. Decide what materials and equipment you need to test your ideas. Then, try them out.

Reflect on Your Results

1. What techniques did you test in step 2?

2. How successful were they?

3. Check with other groups to see what they tried. How do their techniques compare with yours? (What is similar about what they did? What is different?)

4. What new ideas would you like to try? How might you change any of the techniques you used? Try your ideas out.

PART 3: TECHNIQUES FOR PREVENTING SOIL EROSION

These photos show three common ways that farmers and gardeners prevent soil erosion.

1. Do some research to find out how each technique works and where it is used.

▼ terracing

▲ mulching

▼ shelterbelt

What Did You Learn?

Based on your experiences in part 1 and part 2 of Let's Experiment, answer these questions:

1. What difference would it make to the amount of time it takes for all the water to flow out of the eavestrough if you leaned the eavestrough on a steeper angle? a less-steep angle?

2. What difference would it make to the amount of sand that ends up in the dishpan?

3. What difference would it make to the amount of time it takes for all the water to flow out of the eavestrough if you used more water? less water?

4. What difference would it make if you put in more soil? less soil?

5. Based on what you learned in part 3, pick one of the above questions to investigate further. If you prefer, come up with your own question to investigate. Design an experiment, write up your plans, show them to your teacher, and then go for it!

INVESTIGATING FURTHER

Protecting a Sandcastle

People are always using what they have discovered about the environment to invent new ways to control it. Do you remember those sandcastles from the activity in Our Ever-Changing Planet?

Think about what you have learned in this activity, and do whatever you think is necessary to prevent a sandcastle from eroding when you drop straws full of water on it. Try it. How well did you protect your castle?

Rock Stories

Every rock has a story to tell about the history of our planet earth.

However, one family of rocks makes it easier to understand its stories than the other families do.

Use these pictures to help you guess which family of rocks that is. What clues can you use to help you?

In **Getting Started** you will look for stories in rocks. In **Let's Investigate** you will make your own imprint. In **Investigating Further** you can share other rock stories with your class.

GETTING STARTED

Imagine that you are walking through wet cement that has just been poured and smoothed out. You leave a trail of footprints behind you as you walk. When the cement hardens, the imprints of your feet—your footprints—remain. Even 100 years or more after you die, people will know that some young person (you!) walked there. You have left a story in the cement!

Our planet has been a home for millions of different kinds of living things over its long history. How do we know this? We can tell from the stories that sedimentary rocks tell us. Many of these stories appear as imprints left in the rocks.

What story details can you see in each of the photos to the left? For example, what do you think happened to form each imprint, and how do you think it got preserved?

LET'S INVESTIGATE

You will need
- a plastic container such as a 250-mL tub
- some modelling clay
- a dog biscuit or a small, clean bone
- plaster of Paris

In this activity you'll get a chance to make your own imprint. You'll also learn about another way that rock stories are often told.

1. Put enough softened modelling clay in the bottom of the plastic container to form a smooth, shallow layer.

2. Gently press the dog biscuit or the bone into the clay. Then, gently take it out. In your science journal, describe what the clay looks like.

3. Carefully pour some of the plaster of Paris that your teacher has prepared into the dog-biscuit or bone imprint. Give it time to harden. Then, remove the clay and plaster from the container. Carefully peel the clay away from the plaster. In your science journal, describe what you see.

1. An imprint is sometimes called a mould. In which part of this activity did you make a mould?

2. A cast is a copy of something made from a mould. In which part of this activity did you make a cast?

Many rock stories about the earth's history are told in the form of casts. Think about the ways in which they are different from and similar to the rock stories told by imprints as you read the Information Station.

INFORMATION STATION

How Do Fossils Form?

Most **fossils** are traces left by ancient living things that still exist today because they have turned into rock.

If you've ever been to a museum or watched a nature show on TV, you've seen pictures of fossil bones. Did you know that they have become solid rock? In other words, they aren't bone anymore! Over millions of years, all the original bone material was broken down and replaced by minerals mixed in water (like your salt-water mixture). The mineral mixture slowly hardened into solid rock in the exact shape of the original bone.

The middle photograph looks like wood, doesn't it? But it's actually a rock, a fossil. All the original tree material was broken down long ago. The mineral mixture that replaced it hardened into an exact copy of the shape of the original wood.

Sometimes, fossils have most or all of the original parts. (This is rare, however.) One example is amber. It's the hardened sap of ancient trees. In this case, insects got trapped in the sticky sap when it flowed out of the tree.

When you look at amber like this, you're looking at actual animals that may have lived millions of years ago!

SCIENTISTS IN ACTION

Rock hounds love collecting rocks. Some rock hounds are also "fossil fiends"! They're just wild about collecting fossils.

One of the largest collections of fossils in the world is kept in a museum in Ithaca, New York. Many of the fossils in this collection were donated by a "fossil fiend" named Eleanor Bayley. She knew that her fellow "fiends" sometimes had trouble identifying the fossils they found. That's why she made her collection available to the museum—so that other people could try matching their fossils to hers.

fossil human footprints in Tanzania ▼

Bayley is just one in a long line of fossil collectors extending back to the early 1800s. Some of the earliest fossil collectors, in fact, were women. They became experts at recognizing fossils and excavating (unearthing) them.

Unfortunately, women in the 1800s (and even up until recent times) were often discouraged from taking an interest in science. As a result, credit for their work sometimes went to their husbands. For example, a British fossil hunter named Mary Horner became an expert at identifying the fossils of sea creatures. She was married to Charles Lyell (a scientist who helped explain many things, such as weathering and erosion). Lyell incorporated much of Horner's work into his own, so many people gave him credit for her work as well.

Perhaps the most famous woman fossil hunter, Mary Leakey, worked in Africa from the late 1940s until the 1980s. Leakey discovered many important fossils related to human history there. In 1978, she made a startling discovery: fossil human footprints. Scientists believe an ancestor of ours made them over three-and-a-half million years ago!

What Did You Learn?

1. If you were going to search for fossils, in what kind of rock would you look? Give reasons for your answer.

2. Why would fossils be rarer in other kinds of rock?

3. Think about this sentence: "Fossils usually contain the actual remains of things that were once alive." Explain why you agree or why you disagree with it.

One of the best places in the world to learn about fossils is in Canada: the Royal Tyrrell Museum in Alberta. You can visit it on the Internet at http://tyrrell.magtech.ab.ca/home.html.

INVESTIGATING FURTHER

Telling Rock Stories

The stories that rocks tell can be interpreted in many ways. For example, about 40 km south of Calgary, Alberta, lies an 18 000 tonne boulder. Such a big rock has a huge story to tell! Scientists interpret this boulder's story one way. They say that it was transported to its present location by a river of ice (a glacier) about 10 000 years ago. According to Aboriginal people of the Blackfoot Nation, a mighty warrior named Napi chased the big rock to its present location. (There is much more to the story, but you could find that out for yourself.)

Peoples of all cultures have their own ways of reading the stories that rocks tell. Find and share a rock story with your class from your own or another culture. Be sure to tell the story in two ways: the way scientists interpret it and the way storytellers interpret it.

We Depend on Rocks

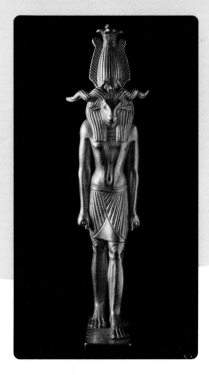

You probably know that people value gold. They have for centuries. Why is gold so special, so valuable? Here are a few of gold's properties:

- soft enough to be pressed or beaten easily into different shapes without breaking
- easily pulled out to form extremely thin wires without breaking
- very good carrier of electricity
- very good conductor of heat
- resistant to weathering
- shiny and beautiful to look at

In Getting Started you will identify things you use that come from rocks or minerals. Then, in Let's Investigate you will gather information about materials that are made of rocks or minerals.

GETTING STARTED

Which of these items comes from rocks or minerals?

The drawings on page 224 show only a few of the many ways in which we depend on rocks and minerals. Each use of rocks or minerals began with a scientific discovery, either about the properties of a rock or mineral or about a new technology. Soon, a use was found for that new knowledge. You can probably think of many other uses for rocks and minerals. How do you depend on rocks and minerals in your daily life?

Did you know, for example, that we use sand and limestone to make glass? These rocks are put in a furnace with certain chemicals until everything melts. While the mixture is liquid, it can be formed into flat sheets, bottles, or any other shape. When the mixture cools, it hardens and keeps the shape it was given. We can then use it for a window, a jam jar, or an optical fibre.

LET'S INVESTIGATE

Are you ready to explore another way of using rocks or minerals?

1. Pick one of the following rock- and mineral-related questions to investigate. You may want to do a little "digging" into some of them first to help you decide which one you'd like to choose. If none of these questions interests you, come up with your own instead. There are lots of possibilities!

- How are roads made?
- How are steel girders for bridges made?
- How are aluminum cans made?
- How is talcum powder made?
- How is pottery made?
- How is plastic made?
- How is toothpaste made?

You will need
- access to information resources such as library books, the Internet, and real experts

For some ideas to help you with your research, look in the Toolkit on page 248.

2. Be sure you look for this information:
- what rock- or mineral-related materials the product contains
- which part or parts of the world the rock or mineral materials come from
- how they are taken out of the ground (mined)
- how they are processed in order to make the product
- what waste materials the mining and processing produces and how these waste materials are dealt with
- what the positive and negative effects of making the product are
- which scientific idea or discovery led to that use for rock or mineral materials
- whatever other interesting information you'd like to share

3. Present your findings in any form you choose. For example, you could make a poster, a labelled diagram, a pamphlet, or a comic strip. Can you think of some other possibilities?

What Did You Learn?

1. Describe one way rocks are taken out of the ground.

2. Pick one thing that is made using rocks or minerals. What rock or mineral is used to make it? Why do you think that rock or mineral is used? What is done to the rock or mineral to make the item?

Thinking About Earth Lab

1. Draw a picture of your classroom or a room in your home. Label five things in the picture made using rocks or minerals.

2. If you had 12 rock samples to sort into groups, what groups would you separate them into? Why?

3. How could you use your fingernail, a copper penny, and a steel nail to help you rank these four things in order from softest to hardest?

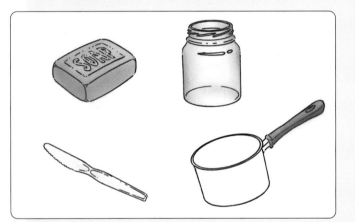

4. Why is it important for a scientist to make careful observations and keep good records?

5. Play a game of "Mystery Rock" with some of your classmates. Use a collection of 10 rocks. Take turns choosing a rock and giving clues about it that the others use to try to guess which rock it is. (Hint: Save the most obvious clues for last.)

6. Imagine that you have just built a house on a steep hill. Draw a picture to show how you would keep the soil around the house from eroding.

7. What story can this rock tell? Share the rock's story with a classmate. What parts of your stories were similar? How were your stories different?

Celebrating Science

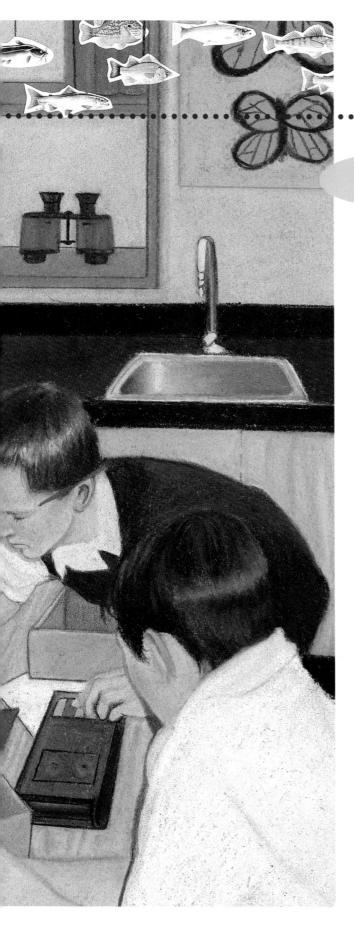

What in this classroom reminds you of the science that you learned this year?

Which tools in the picture did you use?

What did you learn about the life in this classroom?

What investigations did you do?

At the beginning of this book, you were asked to write what you knew about these questions:

1. Why does an Arctic hare change colour in the winter?

2. What sound does a spaceship make in space?

3. How do things get invented?

4. What is a rainbow made of?

5. How are rocks formed?

Find and read your answers in your science journal. What have you learned since you wrote those answers?

Science on Parade

Throughout the year you have learned many things about science and technology. You will be able to use the information you have learned and the skills you have developed in many ways. To celebrate your learning, you are going to work as a member of a team to complete a small project.

GETTING STARTED

Take a few minutes to look through your science journal. Look through this book, too. Write some things you learned about science and technology this year.

Write two sentences that begin: I learned that....

Write two sentences that begin: I learned how to....

Write two sentences that begin: I learned that scientists....

Make a class list to show what everyone learned. Write the "I learned that..." sentences on a list large enough for the whole class to see. Make a list of the "I learned how to..." sentences and a list of the "I learned that scientists..." sentences as well.

LET'S PLAN

What a lot of learning you have done! You can celebrate what you have learned by having a miniature parade. You will work in groups of three or four to make small floats for your parade. Each group will make one float.

In your groups, decide what you would like to celebrate on your float.

1. Read the lists your class made of things they learned.

2. Everyone suggest two possible areas of science to celebrate.

3. Decide which area your whole group would like to work with. If you don't agree, you can vote.

4. Decide together what things you have learned about the area that you could show on your float.

Reflect on Your Results

1. Write a title for your float that tells what your float will celebrate.

2. In what ways did your group work together as a team?

Making Things Move

Now that your group has decided what area to celebrate, you can begin to plan your float for the parade. To make the parade really interesting, each float will have parts that move. What have you learned about making things move?

GETTING STARTED

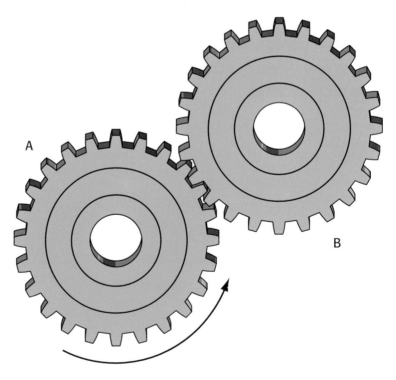

Imagine that gear A is turned in the direction of the arrow. Explain to a partner what gear B will do. Be sure that you and your partner agree.

LET'S EXPLORE

This activity will give you some ideas about how gears and pulleys can help you move things on your float.

PART 1

1. Push six toothpicks into the edges of a slice of potato to make a gear. Be sure the toothpicks are evenly spaced.

2. Push a toothpick through the centre of your gear for you to hold.

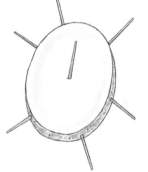

3. Work with a partner. Hold one gear horizontally and one gear vertically with their edges together. Turn one gear. What happens to the other gear?

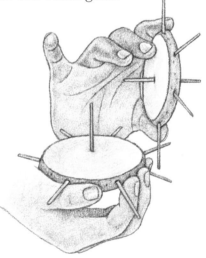

4. Turn the gear in the opposite direction. What happens to the other gear?

5. Try to add a third gear. Predict what will happen if you turn one gear.

6. Try it. How close was your prediction?

You will need

- 1 paper cup
- 7 large paper clips
- sand
- string

PART 2

1. To make a load to lift, fill the paper cup with sand.

2. Open up five paper clips, leaving the hooks on each end.

3. Attach three paper clips around the rim of the cup. Use a fourth paper clip to hook together the other ends of the three paper clips.

4. Tie a string to the top paper clip.

5. Tape another open paper clip to a desk so it hangs over the edge. Run the string through the paper clip.

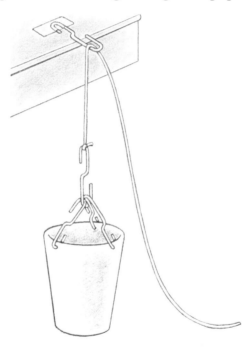

6. Pull on the string to lift the paper cup. Try to remember how hard you had to pull or use a pull-meter to measure how hard you need to pull.

7. Take the string out of the hanging paper clip.

8. Bend two paper clips as shown here.

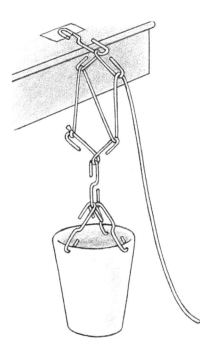

You can use a pull-meter to measure how hard you have to pull to lift the paper cup. For instructions on how to build a pull-meter, see the Toolkit on page 247.

There are lots more ideas for making gears and pulleys in **_The Science Book of Machines_** by Neil Ardley (Doubleday: Toronto, ON, 1992).

9. Put one through the hanging paper clip and one through the top paper clip on the cup.

10. Tie a string to one end of the bent paper clip attached to the cup. Run the string through one of the top loops, then the other bottom loop, then the other top loop.

11. Pull on the string to lift the cup.

12. How was this like using three pulleys?

Reflect on Your Results

1. Which pulley system made it easier to lift the cup—the one with one pulley or the one with three?

2. What can gears help you do?

3. What have you learned about making gears?

4. What can pulleys help you do?

5. What have you learned about making pulleys?

Design Your Float

Think about what you have learned about gears and pulleys. Think about what you are going to celebrate about science. Now it's time to put these two ideas together and design your float!

GETTING STARTED

Here are some guidelines to keep in mind as you design your float.

Your float must be

- 25 to 40 cm long
- 15 to 25 cm wide
- no more than 50 cm tall

It must include moving parts that are powered by an elastic or spring, or by gravity. It must use at least two gears or pulleys.

In your group, brainstorm what you could put on your float to celebrate science. Remember the title you wrote.

LET'S DESIGN

Before building something, it's a good idea to draw up a set of plans and make a list of the materials you require. Follow these steps to design your float.

1. Decide what parts of your float will move. Start with a simple idea. You can always add to it.

2. Decide how to use pulleys and gears to help make the parts move. How will you make the pulleys or gears?

3. Decide how to provide energy to make the pulleys and gears move. There are some ideas in the picture on the next page.

4. Check that your float includes at least two pulleys or gears.

5. Draw a plan for your float. Label the important parts and list the materials you will need to build it. Show this plan to your teacher.

Reflect on Your Results

1. How difficult might it be to follow your plans and construct this float? Why? How long do you think it will take?

2. If you can't find some of the materials you have listed, what could you use instead?

3. What tools might you need to build your float?

4. What methods or materials might you use to fasten parts of your float together?

Time to Celebrate!

The time has come to build your float and celebrate science!

GETTING STARTED

As a group, review your plans for your float. Use your list of materials as a checklist. Decide who will gather which materials. Make a list of the jobs to be done. Decide what construction jobs everyone in the group will have.

LET'S BUILD

1. Gather the materials you will need to build your float.

2. Check your plan to see how large the pulleys and gears should be. Build the pulleys and gears for your float.

3. Build any other part of your float that will need time to dry.

4. Attach the pulleys to the parts of your float that will move. Try them. How well do they work? If necessary, gather the group together to revise the plan so they will work better.

5. Build the other pieces of the float and put them together.

6. Share your float with others. Show them how it works.

Reflect on Your Results

1. How is your float different from what you expected? What ideas did you change as you went along?

2. What would you do differently the next time? What worked well?

3. What science and technology did you learn by making your float?

4. What science and technology did you learn by looking at other groups' floats?

Toolkit

You will need
- interlocking cubes

FINDING AREA

There are several ways to find the area of any shape. Here are two ways.

1. Cover the area you want to measure with identical square shapes, such as interlocking cubes.
2. Count the number of squares that cover the area.

or

1. Place a row of identical square shapes, such as interlocking cubes, along the width of the shape.

2. To help you count how many rows you would need to cover the shape, place a row of squares along the length.

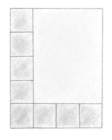

3. Multiply the number of squares across the width by the number of rows you would need to cover the shape. This tells you the area of the shape.

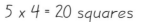

5 x 4 = 20 squares

MAKING A BALANCE

You can construct a working balance using these instructions.

1. Use the tape to attach a tart tin to each end of the ruler.

2. Tape the marker to the table to secure it in place.

You will need
- masking tape
- a ruler
- a round marker or pencil
- a pen
- 2 tart tins or other small, light containers

3. Balance your ruler on the marker.

4. Draw a line on the ruler marking the point where it balances on the marker. Every time you set your balance up, place the line exactly over the marker.

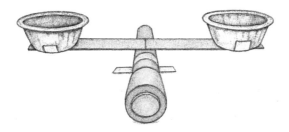

You can then place an object in each tart tin to see which one is heavier.

Using a Balance

You can use your balance to compare the mass of objects.

1. Place one object on each end of the balance and observe what happens.

2. Make a statement about what happened.

Why is it important to make sure the ruler and tart tins balance before you place the objects?

You can measure the mass by using small objects, such as plastic cubes or marbles, as masses. You could also use a set of standard masses.

1. Place the object you are measuring on one end of the balance.

2. Add masses to the other end until it balances.

3. Count the number of small objects you used to balance your object, or add up the standard masses, and make a statement about the mass of your object.

Imagine that you are measuring the mass of an object using a set of plastic cubes. With four cubes on the balance, the end with the object you are measuring is still down. When you place a fifth cube onto the balance, that end goes all the way down. What do you know about the mass of the object you are measuring?

BAR GRAPHS

Bar graphs are a useful way of presenting information you have collected. Anything that you can count, or tally, can be used to make a bar graph.

You will need
- graph paper
- a pencil
- coloured pencils

1. Collect information in your science journal about what you are investigating, for example, the number of bees and the number of ants in the playground.

2. On graph paper, draw one vertical line and one horizontal line that meet. It will look like this.

3. Starting at the bottom, draw a vertical bar made out of squares to show how many things you counted. If you counted two things, make your bar two squares high.

Insects We Saw

4. Draw other bars beside it for the other things you counted. Shade each bar a different colour and label each bar. Give your bar graph a title.

5. For some graphs, when you count 100 or even 1000 things, you will need to make each bar one square high for each 10 or 100 things you count.

LIGHT BOX

You can use a light box to study how a beam of light behaves.

1. With the scissors, carefully cut a hole in one end of the box. Cut from the top all the way down to the bottom.

2. Cut a piece of aluminum foil large enough to cover the hole. Use scissors to cut a small vertical slit in it. You can do this neatly by folding the foil first.

3. Tape the piece of aluminum foil over the hole so that the slit is at the bottom of the box.

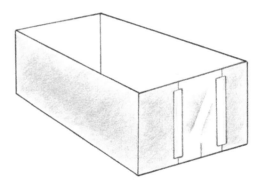

4. Place the flashlight in the box with the light facing the end with the hole.

5. Turn on the flashlight.

Aim the light ray at a mirror. What do you see? How can you change how the light looks?

MAGNIFIER

You can use a magnifier to make small things appear larger.

1. Carefully cut the bottom out of the margarine container.

2. Carefully cut the centre out of the lid, leaving just the rim.

3. Stretch a piece of plastic wrap over the top of the container and hold it in place with the lid.

4. Gently press on the plastic wrap to form a depression of 1 to 2 cm.

5. Remove the lid, but make sure the plastic wrap stays in place.

6. Fill the depression with water.

7. Stretch another piece of plastic wrap over the top to hold the water in place.

8. Replace the lid to hold the plastic wrap in place.

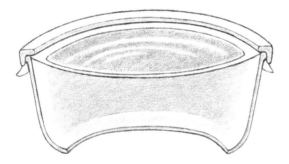

Place the container over anything you want magnified. How might you make this magnifier more powerful?

Using a Magnifier

To see things, we need light and we must have the image in focus.

1. Make sure the object you are looking at is in a bright spot.
2. Hold the magnifier close to the object and then move the magnifier towards your eye. Stop when the image is clear and easy to see.

What happens if you try to look at something through two magnifiers? Try to adjust them so that the image is clear (in focus).

PULL-METER

This device can measure the pull needed to move or lift something.

1. Slip the elastic band onto one of the paper clips.

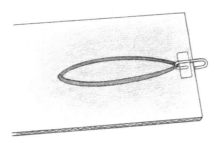

2. Slide the paper clip over the end of the cardboard strip and use the tape to hold it in place.

3. Open the other paper clip so that there is a hook at each end.

4. Hook one end of the opened paper clip through the elastic and squeeze the paper clip closed so that the elastic band is trapped inside.

5. Hold the pull-meter up so that the elastic band lies flat (but isn't stretched). Mark a line and a 0 on the cardboard where the end of the elastic band falls.

6. Use your ruler to mark every centimetre along your pull-meter from 0 to the end without the paper clip. This is called the scale. It will help you tell how hard something is pulling on your pull-meter.

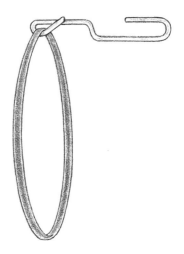

Try it by pulling something or picking something up. How does it work?

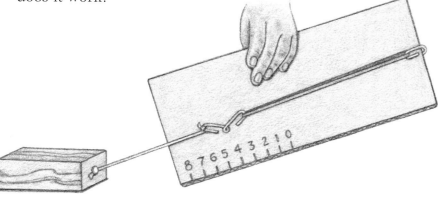

RESEARCHING

When you research information you use many skills. You need to find the information, organize it, understand it, decide what to use, and share it.

These questions can help as you do your research.

1. What topic are you researching?
2. What questions are you trying to answer?
3. Where will you look?
4. Whom might you talk to? phone? write a letter to?
5. What library resources might have information?
6. What key words will help your Internet or library search?
7. How will you record and organize the information you find?

CHOOSING AND USING TOOLS

These tools are useful for building things:

- safety glasses
- drill
- saw with fine teeth
- mitre box and/or vise
- screwdrivers (3 sizes of Robertson—green, red, black)
- various sizes of Robertson head screws
- claw hammer
- various sizes of regular and finishing nails
- clamps

These tools are useful for taking things apart:

- safety glasses
- needle-nose pliers
- adjustable wrench
- precision screwdrivers
- vise

Workbench Safety

- Wear safety glasses or goggles at all times.
- Make sure you have your own work space where you won't hit others with your tools.
- Use tools only for their intended purpose.
- Take your time—don't force the tools or rush.
- Keep your work space clean and tidy.
- Put tools back in their proper storage place.

Glossary

adaptations: the body parts and abilities an animal has to help it survive in its habitat. *White fur is an Arctic hare's adaptation that helps it to hide from its predators.*

camouflage: colours, shapes, and patterns that blend well with an animal's habitat and so make the animal hard to see. *The colour of a frog's skin helps camouflage it from its predators.*

carnivore: an animal that eats other animals. *Lions, wolves, and sharks are carnivores.*

cast: a copy of something that is formed in a mould. *The scientists used plaster to make a cast of the dinosaur footprint.*

community: different populations living in the same habitat. *The pond community includes fish, plants, frogs, and birds.*

consumer: something that eats or consumes other living things. *Animals are consumers.*

erosion: the process by which rocks are worn away and broken into smaller bits, which are then carried away by wind or water. *There was hardly any sand left on the shore because of erosion from the ocean's waves.*

extinct: no longer existing. *Woolly mammoths became extinct thousands of years ago.*

food chain: the path that food energy travels from a producer to a consumer. *When a fox eats a rabbit that ate the grass we have a food chain.*

fossil: living things preserved in rock or some other material. *The broken rock revealed the fossil of a fish.*

gear: a wheel with teeth, grooves, or ridges that connects with another gear and turns it. *Changing gears on a bicycle makes it easier (or harder) to turn the wheels.*

habitat: the natural living or dwelling place of a plant or an animal. *Forests are the natural habitat of the bear.*

herbivore: an animal that eats plants for its energy. *Deer, caterpillars, and chipmunks are herbivores.*

igneous rock: rock that forms when hot liquid magma cools and hardens. *Granite is an igneous rock.*

magma: liquid rock beneath the earth's surface. *When magma flows out of a volcano it is called lava.*

metamorphic rock: rock that forms from already-existing rock that changes because of intense heat and pressure. *When the sedimentary rock called shale is put under pressure it changes to the metamorphic rock called slate.*

mineral: a naturally occurring substance that forms in crystals. *Scientists found minerals that had been embedded in the rock for thousands of years.*

omnivore: an animal that eats both plants and animals. *Bears, raccoons, and humans are omnivores.*

opaque: describes a substance or object that blocks all light from passing through. *The heavy curtains on the window are opaque.*

pitch: describes whether a note is high or low. *The pitch of the note got lower as the vibrations slowed.*

population: the number of similar living things in a habitat. *The population of oak trees in the park is nine.*

predator: an animal that hunts and eats other animals. *Cats are one of the predators of mice.*

prey: an animal that is hunted and eaten by a predator. *Mice are prey for owls.*

producer: something that produces its own food in order to survive. *Green plants are called producers because they make their own food out of sunlight, air, and water.*

property: a quality or feature of an object or substance. *One property of water is that it will freeze at 0˚C.*

pulley: a wheel with a groove that a wire, rope, string, or belt fits into that is used to lift or move things. *The elevator used pulleys to transport people from floor to floor.*

reflection: an image that bounces (or reflects) off a surface. *They saw their reflection in the still water.*

sediment: tiny pieces of mud, rock, or organic material that settle at the bottom of a liquid. *The thick layer of sediment at the bottom of the pond was made of decayed leaves.*

sedimentary rock: rock that is made up of sediment, pieces of older rock, or organic material. *Shale is a sedimentary rock.*

spectrum: the name given to the band of colours that forms when white light passes through a prism. *The colours of light in a spectrum range from violet, through blue, green, yellow, and orange, to red.*

translucent: describes a substance or object that allows some, but not all, light to pass through. *Waxed paper is translucent.*

transparent: describes a substance or object that allows light to pass through. *Glass in a window is usually transparent.*

vibration: a quick back-and-forth movement that creates sound. *The strings on a guitar vibrate when they are played.*

weathering: rocks wearing down and breaking into smaller bits. *Thousands of years of wind, water, and ice had weathered the rocks.*

Acknowledgements

Photographs

Abbreviations: SPL = Science Photo Library, T = Top, B = Bottom, C = Centre, L = Left, R = Right

p. 16: Ontario Hydro; pp. 24-25: NASA; p. 26(TL): Geographical Visual Aids; p. 26(TR): David Nunuk/First Light; p. 26(BR): Geographical Visual Aids; p. 26(BL): Peter Arnold/Peter Arnold, Inc.; p. 29(T): J. Lemire/ Publiphoto; p. 29(B): Jeremy Burgess/SPL/Publiphoto; p. 31(T): Edimedia/Publiphoto; p. 31(B): George Bernard/SPL/Publiphoto; p. 37(TL): Gerard Lacz/Publiphoto; p. 37(TR): J. L. Paumard/Colibri/Publiphoto; p. 37(BL): Gerard Lacz/Publiphoto; p. 41(T): Tom Brakefield/First Light; p. 41(C): Victoria Hurst/First Light; p. 41(B): Gerard Lacz/Publiphoto; p. 48(TL): Geographical Visual Aids; p. 48(TR): Gerard Lacz/Publiphoto; p. 48(BR): David Nunuk/First Light; p. 54(TL): Gordon Petersen/First Light; p. 54 (TR): F. de Pierrebourg/ Publiphoto; p. 54(BR): Warren Faidley/Picture Group/Publiphoto; p. 54(BL): P. G. Adam/Publiphoto; p. 62(T): A. Allstock/Publiphoto; p. 62(B): J. P. Danvoye/Publiphoto; pp. 70-71: Courtesy Canadian Children's Opera Chorus; p. 73(T): Larry J. MacDougal/First Light; p. 73(BL): Y. Beaulieu/Publiphoto; p. 73(BR): G. Zimbel/ Publiphoto; p. 77: R. Lankinen/First Light; p. 79(T): Y. Beaulieu/Publiphoto; p. 79(TC): P. Andrews/ Publiphoto; p. 79(BC): A. Wolf/Publiphoto; p. 79(B): Alan Marsh/First Light; p. 92(TL): Pierre Bernier/ M. E. F./Publiphoto; p. 92(TR): E. Bilderberg/First Light; p. 93: Canapress; p. 113: Eric Cadesky/The Glass Orchestra; p. 115: Courtesy Canadian Children's Opera Chorus; p. 127: U. S. Patent Office; p. 131: Courtesy Canadian Geographic; pp. 138-139: Canada in Stock/Ivy Images; p. 142(T): Benjamin Rondel/First Light; p. 142(C): Ron Watts/First Light; p. 142(B): Bill Ross/First Light; p. 143(T): Gordon Garradd/SPL/Publiphoto; p. 143(TC): D. Woods/First Light; p. 143(BC): Allan Morton/Dennis Milon/SPL/Publiphoto; p. 143(B): R. Maisonneuve/Publiphoto; p. 148: Martyn F. Chillmaid/SPL/Publiphoto; p. 150: Julien Lama/Publiphoto; p. 154: Alan Marsh/First Light; p. 162(T): Denis Roy/Valen Photos; p. 162(BR): Eric Kamp/Phototake/First Light; p. 162(BL): P. Andrews/Publiphoto; p. 166(T): Bruce Berg/Visuals Unlimited; p. 166(BC): Hattie Young/SPL/Publiphoto; p. 172: Dick Hemingway; p. 173(T): John D. Cunningham/Visuals Unlimited; p. 173(B): A. M. Siegelman/Visuals Unlimited; p. 175: Dave Reede/First Light; p. 177: David Parker/SPL/ Publiphoto; p. 182(L): Corbis-Bettman; p. 182(R): Corbis- Bettman; p. 183: Canada in Stock/Ivy Images; pp. 184-185: Y. Derome/Publiphoto; p. 190(TL): S. McCutcheon/Visuals Unlimited; p. 190(BL): Arthur R. Hill/Visuals Unlimited; p. 190(Mineral 1): A. J. Copley/Visuals Unlimited; p. 190(Mineral 2): A. J. Copley/ Visuals Unlimited; p. 190(Mineral 3): H. Berthoule/Jacana/Publiphoto; p. 190(Mineral 4): Arnold Fisher/ SPL/Publiphoto; p. 190(Mineral 5): Dane Johnson/Visuals Unlimited; p. 190(Mineral 6): John D. Cunningham/Visuals Unlimited; p. 191(Rock 1): L. S. Stepanowicz/Visuals Unlimited; p. 191(Rock 2): Kurt Kamin/Visuals Unlimited; p. 191(Rock 3): L. S. Stepanowicz/Visuals Unlimited; p. 191(Rock 4): A. J. Copley/Visuals Unlimited; p. 191(Rock 5): A. J. Copley/Visuals Unlimited; p. 191(Rock 6): Bill Ivy/Ivy Images; p. 191(Rock 7): Michael Long/Visuals Unlimited; p. 191(Rock 8): A. J. Copley/Visuals Unlimited; p. 191(Rock 9): Tom Pantages; p. 191(Rock 10): A. J. Copley/Visuals Unlimited; p. 199(L): Dane S. Johnson/ Visuals Unlimited; p. 199(CL): Ken Lucas/Visuals Unlimited; p. 199(CR): Arthur R. Hill/Visuals Unlimited; p. 199(R): Jeff J. Daly/Visuals Unlimited; p. 201: P. Le Ploche/Explorer/Publiphoto; p. 202: Science/Visuals Unlimited; p. 203(LT inset): Kurt Kamin/Visuals Unlimited; p. 203(RT inset): L. S. Stepanowicz/Visuals Unlimited; p. 203(B inset): L. S. Stepanowicz/Visuals Unlimited; p. 204(LT inset): Bill Ivy/Ivy Images; p. 204(CT inset): A. J. Copley/Visuals Unlimited; p. 204(RT inset): A. J. Copley/Visuals Unlimited; p. 204(B inset): Michael Long/Visuals Unlimited; p. 205(T): A. J. Copley/Visuals Unlimited; p. 205(C): Tom Pantages; p. 205(B): A. J. Copley; p. 208(T): Bill Banaszewski/Visuals Unlimited; p. 208(BL): Derrick Ditchburn/Visuals Unlimited; p. 208(BR): John Sylvester/First Light; p. 212: Chris Harris/First Light; p. 213(T): J. P. Danvoye/ Publiphoto; p. 213(C): Patrick Endres/Visuals Unlimited; p. 213(B): Martin Bond/SPL/Publiphoto; p. 214: National Archive of Canada/PA 139647; p. 215(L): Tom Hanson/Canapress; p. 215(R): Ivy Images; p. 217(TL): D. Cavagnora/Visuals Unlimited; p. 217(R): C. Meyer/First Light; p. 217(BL): R. Maisonneuve/Publiphoto; p. 219(T): Geographical Visual Aids; p. 219(B): Sylvain Grandadam/Publiphoto; p. 220(T): Royal Tyrrell Museum; p. 220(B): Brian Rogers/Visuals Unlimited; p. 221(T): Carlos Goldin/SPL/Publiphoto; p. 221(C): Geographical Visual Aids; p. 221(B): Alfred Pasieka/SPL/Publiphoto; p. 222: John Reader/SPL/Publiphoto; p. 224: R. Boswell/National Geographic/First Light; p. 227(L): Y. Derome/Publiphoto; p. 227(R): Sinclair Stammers/SPL/Publiphoto.

Illustrations

Dorothy Siemens: pp. 28, 42, 43, 64, 65, 143, 148, 155, 161, 168, 173; Kveta: 101, 102, 103, 121, 125, 129, 134; Stephen Taylor: pp. 169, 171, 172, 186, 193, 209, 210, 211; Heather Graham: pp. 34, 35, 49, 69, 230, 233, 234, 235, 238, 240, 241, 244, 245, 246, 247; Greg Douglas: pp. 6-7, 87, 90, 94, 95, 228-229; Deborah Crowle: pp. 8, 12, 14, 22, 23, 47, 55, 56, 91, 105, 166, 167, 176, 232, 243; William Kimber: pp. 9, 11, 15, 17, 18, 20, 155, 157, 163, 164, 165, 170, 180, 237; Steve Schulman: pp. 21, 99; Annette Tavares-Cromar: pp. 27, 33, 56; Malcolm Cullen: pp. 32, 50, 58, 72, 76, 80, 88, 112, 144, 148; Angela Vaculik: p. 59; John Fraser: pp. 81, 82, 83, 92, 100, 104, 124, 125, 132, 133, 136, 137, 200, 203, 204, 227; June Lawrason: pp. 107, 109, 112; Jock MacRae: pp. 107, 116-117, 118, 119, 128, 216, 224; Carl H. Wiens: p. 111; Mary Jane Gerber: pp. 140, 166; Giovannina Colallilo: pp. 146, 153, 154, 158, 159, 160; Henry Van Der Linde: pp. 155, 156, 179.

The authors and publisher would like to thank the following teachers and their students for helping with the development of *Science Everywhere*:

Sue Voll, N. A. MacEachern Public School, Ontario

Pat Campbell, Howard Debeck Elementary School, British Columbia

Jill Detrubide, Michael Wallace Elementary School, Nova Scotia

Lucille Edmundson, Dougall Avenue Public School, Ontario

Terry Forster, Howard Debeck Elementary School, British Columbia

Mary Helen Harrigan, Holy Rosary School, Ontario

Jeff Hillman, Southwood Public School, Ontario

Pat Liffiton, Dougall Avenue Public School, Ontario

Lilli Kenna, Franklin Public School, Ontario

Brenda MacNeil, Michael Wallace Elementary School, Nova Scotia

Wayne Minick, Baden Public School, Ontario

Joyce Tremaine, Dr. Taylor Elementary School, Ontario

Sherry Weese, Gordon McGregor Elementary School, Ontario